Advanced Karate-Do

Concepts, Techniques, and Training Methods
Revised, Expanded, & Illustrated

by
Elmar T. Schmeisser, Ph.D.*
Nanadan, Shotokan Karate-Do
Kyoshi, International Society of Okinawan/Japanese Karate-Do

Master Instructor
Certified by the
American Teacher's Association of the Martial Arts

*Medical Physiology:
Visual electrophysiology and psychophysics

TAMASHII PRESS
an imprint of Tamashii LLC

St. Louis, Missouri USA

Advanced Karate-Do:
Concepts, Techniques, and Training Methods
Revised, Expanded, & Illustrated
by Elmar T. Schmeisser, Ph.D.

Published by:
Tamashii Press
an imprint of Tamashii LLC
St. Louis, Missouri USA

www.TamashiiPress.com

© 2007 by Elmar T. Schmeisser
All Rights Reserved
ISBN 0-911921-35-4

Original Edition
© 1994 by Elmar T. Schmeisser

Neither the author nor the publisher accepts or assumes any responsibility or liability for any personal injuries sustained by anyone as a result of the use or practice of any of the instructions contained in this volume.

Printed in the United States of America

Dedication

To my fellow Students:

The Way is not static and dead;
learn from the old Masters,
do not worship them;
learn from your Teachers,
do not blindly follow them;
learn from your Students,
do not assume you know all the Truth.

Contents

Dedication		3
Preface		7
Chapter 1:	**Introduction**	9
Chapter 2:	**Hip Power**	13
	2.1 Movement Vectors	15
	2.2 Direct and Reverse Rotation	16
	2.3 Power Sequence	18
Chapter 3:	**Stance**	19
	3.1 Definition	19
	3.2 Stance Tension	20
	3.3 Movement	23
	3.4 Impact	25
Chapter 4:	**Focus**	29
	4.1 Breathing	29
	4.2 Muscle Lock	30
	4.3 Power Flow	32
Chapter 5:	**Thrusting and Striking**	35
	5.1 Definition	36
	5.2 Trajectories	36
	5.3 Impact and Focus	39
	5.4 Targeting	42
Chapter 6:	**Kicking**	45
	6.1 Leg Extension	46
	6.2 Sweeps and Blocks	50
Chapter 7:	**Blocking**	53
	7.1 Definition	53
	7.2 Classification	55
	7.3 Circular Shifting	58
Chapter 8:	**Linkage and Breath**	61
	8.1 Kata Examples	62
	8.2 Applications in Kata	65
Chapter 9:	**Timing**	69
	9.1 Combinations	69
	9.2 Opponents	70
	9.3 Ki	71
	9.4 Training	72

Contents

Chapter 10: **Counterattack** — 75
- 10.1 Outside Shifting — 78
- 10.2 Inside Shifting — 79
- 10.3 Snap Shifts — 82
- 10.4 Two-Step Shifting — 83
- 10.5 Retreat — 84
- 10.6 Attack — 85

Chapter 11: **Sparring Tactics** — 87
- 11.1 Evade Backward — 89
- 11.2 Evade Sideward — 91
- 11.3 Thrust Forward — 93
- 11.4 Flow Around — 95
- 11.5 Parry Large — 97
- 11.6 Parry Small — 99
- 11.7 Mutual Attack — 101
- 11.8 Slip Right — 103
- 11.9 Slip Left — 105
- 11.10 Suppress — 108

Chapter 12: **Styles and Methods** — 111
- 12.1 Dojo Sparring — 111
- 12.2 Kata — 112
- 12.3 Emphasis — 113
- 12.4 Rank — 115
- 12.5 Training — 119

Chapter 13: **Psychological Balance** — 121
- 13.1 Training Methods — 125

Appendix A: **Bibliography** — 129

Appendix B: **Dojo Etiquette** — 131
- B.1 Dojo Kun — 134

Appendix C: **Glossary** — 135

Appendix D: **Class Outlines** — 151
- D.1 Beginner — 153
- D.2 Intermediate — 154
- D.3 Advanced — 155

Appendix E: **Rank Test Requirements** — 157

Appendix F: **Kata: In-Breath Forms** — 163

Appendix G: **About the Author** — 201

Preface

It has been over 10 years since the publication of the first edition of this book. In that time, my understanding of karate-do and the basic principles that underlie my training in Shotokan karate has, of course, evolved. Specifically, the influences of the grappling arts (aikido and judo) as well as both the older style of Japanese sword (Gomokawa Kaishinryu iaijutsu and kenjutsu) and the modern (iaido and kendo) have illuminated areas that were to me at least somewhat muddy. It may seem obvious to many Japanese students and instructors that kendo underlay many of the principles in the karate they practice, but Westerners rarely have prior experience of kendo, and so miss this shared baseline. Accordingly, I have added this information specifically, so that the tactics of specifically the JKA style of sparring might be seen in a broader context.

The years of aikido and sword training have also made changes to what is perhaps now becoming a more personal style of karate. It may be inevitable that as one ages, one's karate also "ages," and in the words of folk wisdom, one finds that "age and treachery can overcome youth and strength." I prefer to think of it more that I am becoming more efficient in my movement, and am teaching better as a result. I now teach kata with applications from the start, and teach basic aikido and judo methods along with the purely percussive. I supplement my teaching with classes in kendo and iaido kata and find that students more easily grasp the concept of body unity in movement as a result.

Finally, and perhaps surprisingly to readers of this book, kyudo (Japanese ceremonial archery) has also influenced what I do. In kyudo, the emphasis is on the archer, not the target. If things go awry, one looks to the archer for the reason, not the equipment or the target. Likewise in karate, if things go awry, one should not look to external causes ("you attacked me wrong") but instead to oneself, for failing what I have come to call "Rule One"—Don't Get Hit.

To the list of acknowledgements I would have to add too many names to mention individually, but prominent among them would have to be Tetsuzan Kuroda Sensei (kenjutsu, iaijutsu), Nishio Shoji Sensei (aikido, iaido) and Dan Deprospero Sensei (kyudo). The insights from their lessons have shaped me more than I can describe. I will close this preface by reiterating what I wrote in the preface to the first edition: I do not consider myself a "master" of karate-do. That I have been given ranks and titles is true, but that is from others, and not "for" me. I simply wish to continue to train and to teach my understanding of this martial art as best I can, and hope that this small book will help others.

Preface to the Original 1994 Edition

I do not consider myself a "master" of karate-do, although that word has as many definitions as there are people defining it. Nor am I a "professional karate teacher," if by that is meant one who earns a living from the sweat of fee-paying students. However, I have studied and practiced karate for more than 25 years. Also, I am a neurophysiologist and study the workings of the human brain and mind. Thus I write both as a scientist and as a martial artist. As a scientist, I believe that the traditional experiential methods of training and the psychological states they induce, i.e., "mastership," can be explained in terms of the physiology of the human brain and the physics of movement. Therefore, I propose to give a method for teaching the transition from student to master, seen by one presumably on the path of that transition, and in terms that a Western mind may understand.

My journey has been aided by many sources, some listed in the bibliography, and by many people. First among these is he who started me on this journey, Mr. Hidetaka Nishiyama (9th *dan,* JKA Shotokan). I also must thank Mr. Noriyasu Kudo (5th *dan,* Kodokan judo), Mr. Shigeru Kimura (7th *dan,* Shukokai Shito-ryu), Mr. Leroy Rodrigues (7th *dan,* Shorinji-ryu, ATAMA), Dr. Tom Walker (5th *dan,* aikido), Dr. Lester Ingber (7th *dan,* AJKA Shotokan) and Mr. Tom Koch (4th *dan,* aikido). There are, of course, many others who cannot be named, but who include all those with whom I have trained. May this work be useful to you and your future students.

Chapter 1
Introduction

This revised edition is the result of the inevitable changes that accompany continued practice. My thoughts on training have changed and matured in the 10 years since this book was originally published. While what I wrote in the earlier edition is not "wrong" in any real sense, I think that there are areas in the book where I could have been clearer. In addition, I have become aware of larger inter-relationships between Shotokan karate and the arts of aikido, jujitsu, judo, and most especially, kendo. This latter connection arose only as I compared my training in sparring tactics with the kendo *kata* I learned after the original edition of this book was published. Similar to the experience that accompanied my linkage between aikido techniques and karate *kata* movements was the experience of realizing the fundamental identity between the tactics taught in the 10 formal kendo *kata* and the tactics taught me in sparring classes across the years. As a result, I felt that the original edition of this book had become incomplete, and needed not only a new chapter, but also additions, rewriting, and general updating. To that end, I have added a new chapter to the book as well as expanded other sections that I had been told were excessively dense. I am afraid that the density may have been only slightly lessened by my efforts; nevertheless, I offer this revision in the hope that understanding may be made easier by it.

That being said, it is still true that there are a multitude of books describing the individual physical techniques of karate for the beginning student. In terms of my understanding of the "way" of karate, it is somewhat irrelevant which one the student chooses—whether it is *kung-fu*, classical Japanese hard style karate, or even one of the American eclectic self-defense or tournament styles. Eventually, if pursued long enough, learning manual techniques for either homicide or for trophy gathering becomes a shallow and meaningless goal. Alternatively, there are philosophical treatises on the martial arts, written by acknowledged masters of both Zen and the individual arts from the point of view of a master. At this level, what is written can be somewhat difficult for the Western mind to understand.

This book is a set of observations, hints, exercises, and ways of thinking about the various technical and mental aspects of karate gleaned from almost three decades of experience in the martial arts. This has been organized into a logical structure or classification scheme that analyzes the physical techniques in a common language related to their forces and dynamics. Also, I have tried to indicate in the same manner at least the first steps needed towards realizing the *kensho* (Zen type of enlightenment) of the martial arts. These thoughts have grown from "bull sessions" with senior instructors from many styles, usually late at night after several beers, and from various arts including such esoteric ones as Zen archery (*kyudo*) and tea ceremony (*cha-no-yu*). Additionally, much material was worked out with students across the years. The basic physical and psychological principles in this book are universal to all the Japanese martial arts; however, due to limitations both of space and my experience, I will use as explicit examples mainly the techniques of karate-do. Very little of the material written here is spoken of in the existing textbooks on karate, which tend to emphasize the physical aspects of individual techniques rather than the theoretical foundation of the art. The published literature reflects its sources: a relatively random collection of historical methods combined with an overlay of modern non-contact tournament techniques. What I have written in this book is aimed at the new instructor (at least *shodan*, although senior brown belts may be forced into teaching roles as well) to aid in the development of a unified way of thinking about technique and training. This should help the instructor to reason from first premises rather than be forced to give only previously heard and memorized answers to questions from his students. I have not given exhaustive examples but only enough to illustrate my points. Nor is the coverage complete in the sense that this book exposes all the "secrets;" learning does not stop. More poetically, perhaps, this book is a small gate, not the full mansion. Further, it is presumed that the reader already has a strong foundation of technical knowledge in karate. Such information is published elsewhere, e.g., in Nakayama, M.: *Dynamic Karate* (see Bibliography).

Readers of the drafts of this book have called the text dense and difficult to read. I offer no apology, but I do recognize that this may be difficult material. It has been written as a reference book rather than a storybook. Perhaps the best strategy is, after a swift first reading, to reread the book, but only one paragraph (or even one sentence) at a time. Between each new concept, the reader should close the book and practice for a day, trying to see where the ideas fit into the current understanding of what is being done both with and to the body and the mind. Only then move on, making personal notes to be used for the time when the reader must stand in front of a class and teach.

One thing should be kept in mind: If a technique is practiced intensively but incorrectly, the trainee will become very good at doing it very wrongly; the errors will become ingrained and very difficult to correct. First, understand the movements; second, visualize them as clearly as possible; then only apply gradually increasing effort in the training. While there are differences in the execution of individual techniques resulting from unavoidable differences in each student's body structure, there are certain principles that are basic to all movement, and these should not be violated. Correct large errors first, and make sure they stay corrected. Details come later—power *much* later. Power and speed arise from correct technique, not the other way around. The desire to apply too much strength too early (mistaking this for power) is almost universal in beginners; advanced students also need to be reminded to avoid this.

Improvement of technique should be undertaken in small, easily handled steps and always preceded with repetitions that are smooth and designed to develop a "groove" or clean habit pattern for each movement.

When combination techniques start to break down from fatigue, simplify the exercise and keep working. This remains true even during "special training." Occasionally, a teacher will push the students beyond their apparent physical limits. Such training has two purposes: (1) the development of physical strength and (2) pushing the students' spirit so that they will realize an ability to surpass any arbitrary level in their development as well as recognize that the mind will generally try to quit long before the body itself would. The instructor must be sure that the movements always conform to correct principles of body mechanics despite the fatigue of the extended training.

Beware of this, however: It is easy to get caught in a net of words and believe one understands. This quickly can become self-delusion. The proof of understanding is not in the ability to repeat sonorous phrases and mystical terms, but in the real world of doing. Karate-do is rooted in the physical world of effects; a mistake will result in a very real bloody nose or a broken rib. For this reason, Asian training methods generally have avoided words and emphasized training. It is the experience of teachers in these arts that too much explanation often inhibits proper training. The only proof of understanding is in practice, and only continued and varied practice can deepen this understanding.

Students may get discouraged with the apparent endless repetition, year to year, of the same basic techniques, but this is due usually to a misperception that nothing about them or their approach to the technique has changed. A useful image to give to the students is that of an ascending spiral—imagine all the basic techniques arranged in a circle through which the class progresses from *kyu* test to *kyu* test across the years. When the next session begins, the techniques are revisited, but this time each student will have advanced so that what is practiced with that technique will change, making it a new practice with different lessons to be learned. If the instructor can encourage this view of basic practice, boredom and the subsequent loss of effort largely can be mitigated. The ability to motivate is one of the hallmarks of a good instructor and does not depend on (although it can be aided by) the ability to outperform any particular student. This becomes especially important as the instructor ages and accumulates injuries, eventually losing the finely honed athletic, competitive, tournament edge developed during the early years of training. The aging process can be slowed with continued training, but it is inevitable. The ability to coach students, however, does not diminish, and in fact should increase with greater experience.

What I espouse in these pages is a "traditional" hard style of karate as opposed to some more modern forms of karate. Specifically, this book is about the Shotokan style of Japanese karate.

The difference between traditional karate and modern karate is perhaps best indicated by the difference in attitude during training: Traditional schools emphasize self-improvement and self-realization as the primary goal, with "not losing" (in an actual fight) as the result of sincere training. Modern tournament schools emphasize being better than others, i.e., winning (and displaying) trophies.

Fun is not the purpose of karate-do; the development of good character is. To the extent that one has ego-centered fun at the expense of others, one has left the realm of *shugyo* ("austere training"—implying self-improvement) behind. On the other hand, training should not be distasteful; it has the rewards of happiness, fascination, satisfaction, and even humor.

Chapter 2
Hip Power

The very heart of the Shotokan style of karate power generation (as in most martial arts) is the movement of the center of mass of the body, generally called the *tanden*. *Tanden* refers to the point a few inches below the navel in the center of the body. Occasionally the term *hara* will be used as well, referring to the entire area within the pelvic basin. There is a tremendous emphasis on thinking of all techniques as not only starting in this center (both mentally as well as physically) but also deriving their driving force from its movement. All combinations of techniques must be tied together into a unified sequence here. All breakdowns in a combination's flow are traceable to a loss of control of this point between movements. Also, breathing must be concentrated here, i.e., abdominal, so as to prevent the center of gravity rising with the shoulders as occurs with normal chest breathing. This concept of belly breathing coordinated with an abdominal center of technique control is universal in the Asian martial arts.

Consider that the image of the Asian strong man emphasizes the hip and belly musculature over the upper arms and chest (compare a *sumo* wrestler with a Greco-roman wrestler, or a *judoka* with a gymnast).

In the following sections are simple statements of the primary axioms that underlay the generation of power. These need to be repeatedly emphasized in training.

As a physical point in space and time, the body center has the possibility of linear movement in three primary directions (see fig. 1): **left and right**, such as used in sliding side elbow attacks and side thrust kicks; **forward and back**, such as used in stepping punches and front thrust kicks; and **rising and sinking**, such as used in dropping vertical elbow attacks and stamping kicks.

Also there are the circular rotations around each of these axes: around the vertical in a horizontal plane (***traversely*** around the spine) or "normal" flat hip rotation, such as used in counterpunching; around the horizontal axis through the hips or ***forward-pendular*** (movement like a pendulum), such as used in front and back kicks; and ***lateral-pendular*** around the belly button axis, such as used in side snap kicks. Normally, movement is along several of these directions at once. For example, a side thrust kick combines a lateral shift (stance leg pressure) with both lateral-pendular (hip lift) and flat (corkscrew path) hip rotations in order to generate impact power.

2.1 Movement Vectors

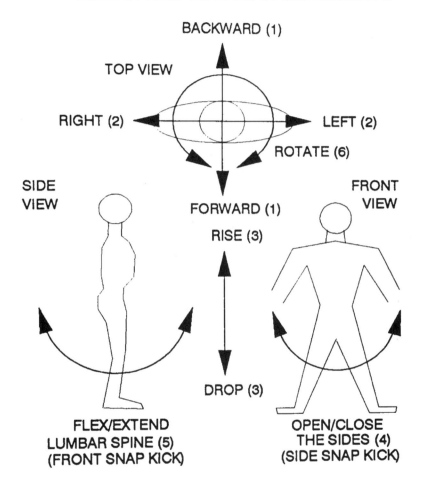

Figure 1
Axes of Motion

The lines and arcs show body movements as follows:
1) linear in X: stepping forward or back (stepping punch);
2) linear in Y: side shifting (lateral elbow attacks);
3) linear in Z: rising and dropping (dropping elbow smash);
4) circular around X: pendular to the side (side snap kick);
5) circular around Y: pendular to the front or back (front snap and back kicks);
6) circular around Z: horizontal hip turning (counterpunch).

2.2   Direct & Reverse Rotation

With the "flat" rotation in particular, but also to a lesser extent with the others, there are two ways to couple a technique to the hips: ***direct*** and ***reverse***. These two ways of coupling power refer to the relationship between the direction of rotation of the body center and the direction of extension/rotation of the limb executing the technique. If both move in the same direction, the coupling is direct; if in opposite directions, reverse. For example, in left foot forward front stance counterpunch position, two middle blocks can be executed with the left hand—the outside and the inside forearm blocks. Both blocks take the hip from front facing (*shomen* or square hips) to half-front facing (*hanmi* or 45 degree slanted hips). In the outside block case, the left arm is moving clockwise as is the hip; thus the hip is providing power in a direct rotation mode. In the inside block, the arm (elbow) is moving counterclockwise while the hip is moving clockwise. This produces a feeling of throwing the technique away from the opposite hip while expanding the chest and connecting across the back. This is reverse rotation.

Most counterpunches are thrown with direct rotation from half-frontfacing to full-front facing. Lead-hand punches are also direct rotation, but with the body moving from front facing to the half-front facing position.

Backfist snaps (see Figure 2) can be thrown either by direct rotation (moving into the technique) or by reverse rotation (spinning the hips away from the fist).

All techniques linked by rotation to the hip have direct and reverse modes, although some are more efficient in one or the other mode and are therefore preferentially executed one way. This linkage must also be made explicit in practice.

TOP VIEWS OF BACKFIST STRIKES

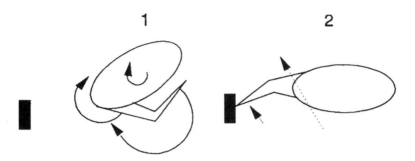

A: Direct Rotation: Body and hand rotate in the same direction

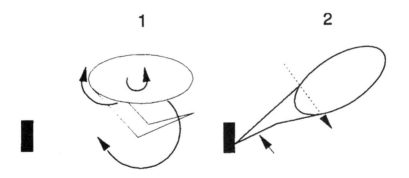

B: Reverse Rotation: Body rotates away from hand

Figure 2
Hip Connection

The two forms of connection to hip rotation are:
(A) direct, as in a weighted back-fist smash; hips turn from half to full facing as the lead hand strikes.
(B) reverse, as in an unweighted back-fist strike; hips turn from full to half facing, throwing the lead hand away from the body center at the target.

2.3   Power Sequence

All physical techniques have an identical time flow to them, moving through three phases. These are 1) *initiation* (or generation), 2) *acceleration*, and 3) *impact* (including the concept of focus).

Initiation is a function of the hips and stance, and it is the impulse that gets everything moving. It incorporates both the initial settling of the feet and toes into the floor, and the contraction of the thigh, buttock, and belly muscles to begin the movement of the major mass of the body. The sharper this phase is, the swifter the whole technique becomes. If this phase is slow, the technique will be slow. More importantly, a slow start will telegraph the technique to the opponent, no matter how efficiently the succeeding phases are performed.

Acceleration can feel almost like coasting or surfing. During this time the momentum generated by the large body muscles is being transferred to the striking limb. The muscles that oppose the movement are kept as relaxed as possible while still keeping the limb on a controlled course. The limb muscles that actually extend the technique are activated in sequence, from the center of the body outwards. This produces a feeling of an expanding and accelerating wave of power. The pullback side of the body is the primary driver for this phase of the technique.

The ***impact*** phase concludes the sequence with a focus of both mental and physical energy into the target. It may include a voiced *kiai* to coordinate the breathing with the rest of the technique. It also includes the controlled release of the accumulated muscle tensions after the focus to allow smooth entry into the following techniques. Punching without a target, i.e. into the air, requires a further component: that of "catching" the limb—so that the joints do not hyperextend—by sharply contracting the antagonist muscles at the point of imagined impact. This also is an aspect of "focus" and is often overemphasized to the detriment of useable technique.

Aspects of each of these phases will be dealt with in the following sections on stance, focus, and thrusting and striking. While they are taught as separate things, in reality they all unite into one power flow from the floor into the target, and it is this unified feeling of flow that produces the most efficient, as well as beautiful, technique.

Chapter 3
Stance

Stances have defined, in a sense, the Asian martial arts to the popular mind, albeit in a very distorted fashion. A person seen on a TV program squatting as if suffering from constipation while emitting hisses, whoops, and various shrieks, is immediately recognizable as performing "karate" or "kung-fu." Add to this some esoteric finger-wiggling combined with stilted English grammar, and we have a media "master." None of this has anything to do with stances, and especially not what they are or how they work. This image must be cleared from students' minds, and the concept of stances demystified and made a natural part of their daily awareness.

3.1 Definition

A stance is no more and no less than a directed pattern of muscle tensions in the hips and legs braced against the floor. Here, training and application must be clearly differentiated.

Training stances are usually large, low, and somewhat exaggerated so that the student can gain flexibility and strength. Training stances are discrete and few in number so the student can gain clarity of internal muscle (proprioceptive) feedback to know where the feet are without looking at them (or in some cases, for them). Additionally, certain techniques are habitually coupled to certain stances for the purpose of linking the upper and lower body; these are neither sacred nor exclusive.

In application, e.g., in free sparring or self-defense, all stances are on a continuum and smoothly blend one into the other. Any particular stance exists only for a fraction of a second, most obviously at the instant of a technique's focus.

Consider the following sequence made by pulling back the front leg: Front stance, rooted stance, back stance, short hourglass stance, cat stance, crane stance, twist stance, (reverse) front stance. Perform the sequence by letting the feet and hips shift smoothly without tension as if drawing a piece of paper along the floor with the toes, (itself a useful exercise in general), and it will become exceedingly difficult to determine where one stance ends and another begins. Excess rigidity will prevent movement completely. Ankle and hip joint flexibility must be an integral aspect of stance training so that stance changing is as easy as normal walking.

To reiterate, discrete stances are for training, but the muscle tensions learned must be applied to any position of the feet and hips. One must be able to "root" at any time and in any position in order to generate the hip rotations and hip thrusts necessary to produce powerful, instantaneous techniques. One cannot wait to counter an attack until one "gets ready."

3.2   Stance Tension

The muscle tensions of the legs in a focused stance, i.e., static and at impact, are of two types—*lateral* and **rotational**. Lateral pressures separate or close the distance between the legs; rotational pressures twist the feet circularly in or out against the floor. These extra tensions do not exist while simply standing in the stance; they occur only when moving some component of the body (for example, the hips) or when accepting some shock back into the body, i.e., impact. When the body is not under stress, that is when one is not initiating a movement or receiving an impact, the legs must be relaxed as far as is consistent with maintaining the position. Especially the feet must be relaxed and the ankles bent, with the feeling of sinking softly into the floor, but without collapsing the knees.

For example, have the student assume a relatively narrow side stance while tucking the hips somewhat under. If the knees and feet are turned-inwards by rotating the thighs so that the heels feel as if they are going to slip outwards while simultaneously the knees come together, one has an hourglass stance (*sanchin*). If the heels are pulled in with the toes immobile and the legs and bent knees pushed apart, one has the classical side stance. Back stance uses outside rotational tensions like side stance, but the lateral tension can be either compressive or expansive, depending on application. Cat stance has inside squeezing (compressive) tensions, but the rotational tensions are very soft and can twist the knees either towards or apart from each other, again depending on what technique it must support. Front stance has outside tension and separating pressure in the Shotokan style, but closing pressure in Shorinji-ryu even though the outside twist is maintained. All the stances should be explored and analyzed as to their component tensions so that awareness of them is heightened to the point that if one were wearing baggy pants, one could shift between a narrow front stance through a back stance to an hourglass stance, and it could not be detected from outside by sight alone. Only the tensions would be different, and thus the techniques that could be powered from them also would change.

One other very important tension is required for a focused stance: that of the link between the legs—the hips and buttocks. It is this final tension that is the critical factor in unifying the lower body and linking it to the upper torso. It is a combination of the Kegel exercise of the pelvic floor muscles in the perineum (including contraction of both the urethral and anal sphincters) and the clamp with the buttocks one involuntarily finds oneself doing in cases of diarrhea (contraction of the gluteus muscles). This not only locks the legs together, but also pushes the hips forward so that the leg-hip joint lies on a plane intersecting the center of both feet. The buttocks muscles are not necessarily equally tense in all stances either, but one side will be preferentially tensed, depending on whether the hips are square on or half-facing.

Unless the spine is straight, i.e. stretched vertically with the shoulders placed directly over the hips both laterally and frontally and the head centered between the shoulders, the shoulders will precess or swing out of the vertical plane with hip rotation, throwing off both balance and power. If all other tensions in the legs fail from fatigue, the ones in and around the pelvic basin must not, or the stance will fall apart and will not support the flow of power into or the reaction back from the target. And this must be practiced because these muscles are weak in chair-sitting Westerners. Sitting (*seiza*) and standing in the Japanese manner requires these muscle tensions with proper alignment for graceful movement, which getting into and out of chairs does not. Additionally, long hours of breath "focusing" by suddenly stopping an exhalation and/or *kiai* without closing this "hole" at the bottom of the body cavity will go far in producing hemorrhoids from the raised internal pressures produced by the contraction.

SIDE STANCE POSITIONING

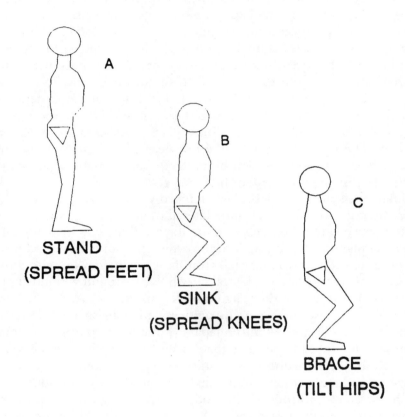

Figure 3
Side Stance

A: Side View of hips and leg in normal standing position, showing the double curve of the spine;
B: Separate the legs and sink into side stance, but without pulling the hips under;
C: Soften the backbone sway-back curvature by slightly tucking the hips with the stomach muscles but without either hunching the back or hollowing the stomach. Move the body center forward so that the hip joint lies over the center of the foot rather than over the heels.

3.3 Movement

How these leg tensions interact with the floor is important for both stance shifting and stepping. It is very easy to lose all tension in the legs while stepping forward so that the step is more of a push-off by the back foot followed by a headfirst fall forward than a swift and balanced movement. This results in the body losing its centered balance (the weight set securely on the hips, which are in turn braced well on the legs), and both mental and physical control.

The usual symptom of this is the raising of the heels and/or the insertion of "cheat steps" at the start of the movements. This action must be eliminated, both by thinking of the initial starting of a step as a pulling together of both legs rather than a push off from one, and by keeping weight on the whole foot rather than only on the toes. One needs to be aware that there is nothing in or on the floor that can be "gripped" by the toes, unless it is a shag carpet. Any attempt to do so will simply arch the foot upwards and reduce contact with the floor. Gravity is the only force that provides the contact pressure; one cannot increase one's weight by tightening the toes.

This feeling of using the whole foot as a platform can be practiced by having the students first stepping with the toes of the anchor foot raised off the floor to emphasize the heel as being the anchor for the pull, then thinking of the hips as moving forward as the toes apply pressure to maintain balance before the lead leg changes from pulling to pushing into the next stance. After this exercise is mastered as an over-correction, simply moving naturally will use the whole foot as the anchor. The traveling foot also should remain parallel to the floor throughout the step, i.e., not droop or point downward throughout its travel.

Further practice can be obtained by stepping slowly forward while having a graded resistance to the step provided by a partner holding the stepping student's hips back with a belt. In this exercise (dubbed "plowhorse" training), the pair moves across the dojo floor, the first pulling the second along. Alternatively, the same resistance can be felt by doing single step forwards with the stepping foot attached to a set of bicycle innertubes fixed behind the trainee as an elastic restraint. In each case, emphasis must be given to having the leg and hip muscles do all the work, avoiding the tendency to lean into the step, and in having the whole foot stay in relaxed contact with the floor rather than simply tightening the toes. Having the foot too tense will result in reduced contact with the floor and slipping of the stance as well as increased vulnerability to foot sweeps.

Alternatively, moving can involve not stepping, but slide-shifting. In this case, the initial movement is a separating of the legs rather than a closing, and requires a strong pressure with the big toe of the anchor foot but without raising the outside edge of that foot. A slide forward requires shifting from a neutral or inside tension stance to outside tension for motion. By contrast, stepping proceeds directly with inside tension pulling the legs together. Movement backwards requires the mental feel of the middle of the back at the chest level as moving backward rather than the hips (to avoid jutting of the buttocks). Stepping backwards has the same feeling of the heels rather than the toes pulling, although the toes must contact the floor for good balance as well as good traction.

In other words, swift starting motion in stepping depends on the lead foot "rooting" and inside tension between the thighs. This is not to be confused with the tension required for finishing motion (impact focus), which is outside-rotational and roots with the back foot using mainly the big toe and the outside edge as the anchor and the front foot as the brake.

3.4 Impact

The final touchstone of any stance is whether or not it will work, i.e., will it support the technique that is based on it during impact? Any impact of an anatomical weapon (fist or foot) on a target will produce a reaction force through the body, which, if the stance is not soundly based, will make the technique (and the person) simply bounce off rather than penetrate the target. The Shukokai school of Shito-ryu karate explicitly makes this reaction force from the target a part of its central rationale. Essentially, power transmission is weakened and power lost at any joint that is bent. This loss is directly in proportion to the amount of bend, the amount of muscle tension around the joint, and the amount of power carried through that joint. Thus the impossible ideal is a straight line from the floor through the leg, hip, back, shoulder, and arm to the fist. Nevertheless, it is essential that at focus, the support (back) leg be stretched as straight as possible and the waist tensed to hold the backbone straight. This can be accomplished with punching techniques by tensing the buttock on the side of the punch. With counterpunch and square hip stepping punches, the buttock of the back leg upon impact is tensed; with flowing and slanted hip lead-hand punches, the buttock under the lead hand is tensed. In all cases, any sharp "corner" in the line of transmission of power from the floor will result in loss of the reaction force from the target back out through the bend, with subsequent loss of impact.

In some cases (e.g. uneven ground) this ideal is impossible to attain, as some bend is needed to maintain both flexibility and balance; attacks made from such "softer" compromise bases will have less impact on their targets. One of the most common compromises, especially seen in competitive free sparring, is the use of momentum to provide the support for a thrusting attack.

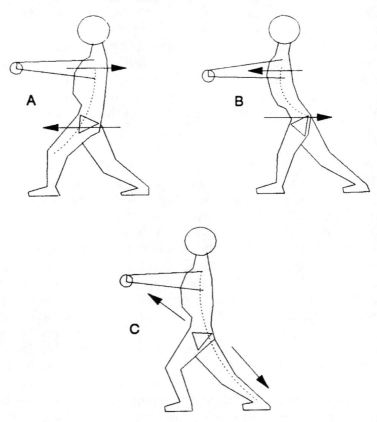

Figure 4
Front Punch

A: too much stomach tension producing a rounding of the back and a collapsing of the stomach muscles (hollowing);
B: too much back tension jutting out the hips (leaning forward);
C: balanced tensions allowing a smooth coupling of the floor to the technique with stretching of the back leg.

Again, this is a compromise with speed in which the forward movement of the body weight is used to provide the impact mass or a "pseudo back leg" for the stance. Physically, it is a one-legged stance, and the reaction force is permitted to dissipate by relaxing the thrust immediately after impact. This technique is useful either when deep penetration of the target is not required (hence its use in tournaments) or with sharp snapping strikes. It remains a non-ideal method, and if used in a serious situation, can surprise the user with its ineffectiveness if the opponent's body is athletically hardened. Further, while purely ballistic strikes and thrusts (if they land) can be effective, without a stance, if they miss, can result in an untenable posture.

The only cure is extended *makiwara* (padded punching board or post) and heavy bag practice to make sure that as much power as can be generated is in fact present. Mere air punching will only produce pretty rather than effective technique. *Makiwara* practice also will correct the looseness produced by too much tournament-style free sparring and will build the impact coordination needed to make a sliding-in counterpunch actually work.

Chapter 4
Focus

Focus (*kime*) is a multidimensional term incorporating aspects of concentration, sight, muscle tensions, and breathing. To some extent, it is a mistranslation of the Japanese term, which implies a more mental process of decisiveness rather than a physical act. However, the common usage denotes a physical expression of this mental state, and applies to the terminus of a technique, its impact phase. In some dojos, it is "taught" to beginners by kicking them in the stomach. While this produces a nominal development of the stomach muscles as well as the ability to *kiai* from the gut, it is only about a third of a complete focus. An excess of such training, in fact, eventually can destroy the ability to transmit power into a target by making the students concentrate more on their own ability to take an impact than to deliver it.

4.1 Breathing

To take the elements in reverse order, breathing is important to focus, but not in the form that sometimes is seen in popularizations of karate. A good focus does not have a long, drawn-out shriek that wails off into the distance.

The voiced shout (*kiai*) is a training method for focus, but *kiai* and yelling are very different things. A yell ends when it runs out of air, getting softer and weaker at the end; a *kiai* is cut short in the throat (glottis) and stops with the maximum muscle tension at impact. The air release (exhalation) in focus is very carefully controlled, and is time-locked to the technique's expansion and compression. In classical Japanese sword training, only three syllables are permitted for *kiai*: "eh," "ya," and "toh." Each of these syllables is voiced with a strong start and a strong stop, but they are subtly different in how they connect the body and how they link to both the technique invitation and impact. In karate, each person must experiment individually, since each body is different, but in no case should the word "kiai" itself be used as a *kiai*. Not only is it equivalent to shouting the word "shout," but it also has two syllables with a weak transition.

A unique characteristic of breathing control as applied in the martial arts is that it is thought of as leading rather than following the technique. In swimming or running, the breath is usually synchronized to the movements, but this synchronization does not mean that the breath itself is considered to be anything other than the method used to oxygenate the muscles. In weight lifting, the thought of "blowing" the weight up with the breath is more common; in karate, the breath is considered the master of the technique.

In other words, inhalation and exhalation are tied to the expansion and contraction of both the body center (belly breathing) as well as extension and retraction of the limbs. This gives the feeling of the body center working as a pump, with its rhythm timing the flow of techniques.

Therefore, considerable emphasis is placed on abdominal rather than thoracic breathing to help forge the link between diaphragmic motion and limb motion. Since it is impossible to focus the body into an impact on an inhalation (one can thrust while inhaling, but it will be a somewhat weaker technique since the upper and lower body cannot be as strongly coupled), sequential focused techniques must either be locked during one segmented out-breath, or have in-breaths between them. The first method involves partially emptying the lungs, closing off the glottis for the first focus, reopening the glottis, and resuming the ex-halation to the next focus. If there is sufficient time, a small inhalation can be squeezed into the time after the first focus.

Thus, an outside block followed by counterpunch can have two focuses in one breath. This requirement for breath control of the techniques imposes limitations both on the length and syncopation of combination attacks as well as on the possibilities for making combinations.

4.2   Muscle Lock

Muscle tensions are another component of focus, especially important in "air" punching (punching without a resistive target that one can actually hit); however, the stomach muscles are only part of the story. The stance, the muscles in the floor of the pelvis (externally, the perineum), the buttocks, and the back and sides of the body also must cooperate, or there is no focus. Moreover, the tensions must be such that power is projected outwards along the attacking limb and down into the floor, rather than pulled back into the body. Several things must happen in a focus:

> 1) The four limbs must be seated into their sockets (shoulders held down while the elbows are kept rotated

inwards so that they point more downward rather than outward; legs are tied together with tensed hip and buttocks), and the muscles around the joints used in their extension locked to prevent hyperextension. The limbs and body actually will get thicker at the moment of focus.

2) The perineum including anal and urethral sphincters, the back muscles of the spine, the side muscles of the torso, the chest, and belly must tighten to increase the intracavity muscular pressure in the body and lock the upper and lower body together.

3) The glottis in the throat must be closed to prevent the air in the lungs—which is being squeezed by the body wall and pelvic muscles—from continuing to escape.

The end result is that the body core forms a pressurized "hydrostatic skeleton" that firmly connects the floor to the target during the extension of the attack. The feeling is that the body actually becomes more compact during the focus. Note that this does not mean hunching down, but an even and proportional compression. Moreover, the feeling is kept that the body center drops down and forward for the impact into the target, and that the attacking limb is squeezed toward the target rather than simply thrown toward it.

This is where stance and breathing unite.

These tensions, of course, must be instantaneously released to permit movement to the next technique. In fact, the tensions around the limb joints that counteract the limb's extension should not even be generated if the technique actually lands on target. Tensions in the body wall must be evenly counterbalanced so that the belly does not overpower the back, or the backpressure from the glottis overpowers the perineal muscles. In the first case, the back rounds over, throwing the technique off and preventing transmission of momentum into the target; in the second, one can demonstrate a disconcerting ability to release lower intestinal gas instead of *kiai* with the technique. The Goju-ryu *kata*, *Sanchin*, specifically trains this form of muscle coordination by dynamic tension, i.e., using slow motions with opposing muscles co-contracting to provide an internal resistance to movement. Combined with breathing also under dynamic tension to strengthen the diaphragm (*ibuki* breathing), this *kata* is one of the best methods to teach this aspect of focus.

4.3 Power Flow

The dynamic flow of power to the focus in the target can be split into two different methods that anchor a continuum—**synchronous termination** of parts and **sequence of joints**. The first *(synchronous termination)* generates power by adding up linear accelerations from each part, and it creates the focus by stopping and locking all the moving elements (legs, hips, shoulders, fist) at the same time. This is normally seen most effectively in short, stocky, "brick-like" bodies.

The other method *(sequence of joints)* is best developed in long, lanky, tall persons, and consists of not only starting the joints in sequence, i.e., legs first, then hips, then chest, then fist, but also stopping each in sequence so that the conservation of angular momentum forces a "whiplashing" of the fist into the target. In essence, this is a separation in time between the generation of the driving power and the acceleration of the fist. This whiplash is not only a vertical sequence from the floor into the target, but also a horizontal sequence in, for example, reverse punch. First, the side opposite the technique hand is pushed at the target, then stabilized there as an anchor; next the technique side is rotated around the set side (note: not around the center of the body) to whip the fist out. Absolutely critical to this technique is that there is no power or muscle tension in the arm before the focus; otherwise it cannot fly freely.

The same sequencing is applied to kicking techniques as well.

The exact amount of temporal asynchrony in the sequential links for the technique depends on where one's individual body type falls in the continuum from blocky to lanky. The only way to determine this is by practicing both extremes of punching form (i.e., synchronous termination and sequence of joint styles) and then finding the personally most efficient compromise.

Hunching the back and collapsing the stomach can ruin the entire flow of power into the target. To correct this, one must feel a compensatory arch both lengthwise along the spine (but without projecting the buttocks backwards, which produces a "corner" or angular break between the spine and the back leg), and across the shoulder blades, thus pushing the chest into the technique and keeping the arms from disconnecting at the shoulders (a "big" chest, but without hollowing the pit of the stomach). Essentially, the image is that of a strut (an arm) braced on the convex side of an arch (the spine), rather than on the concave side (see again fig. 3).

Lastly, a bent knee and a collapsed, tensed stomach will make a punch feel stronger to the person doing it. This is simply because the power is being bounced around internally rather than being transmitted into the target. With truly effective hitting, almost no shock will travel back down the arm. Simply strike a sandbag repeatedly to feel this: It is only when the arm can hit the target without flinching, i.e., relaxed and with the focus locking in only for a moment, that the bag will develop a pocket as the power is sent into the sand. The focus must always be outwards into the target, never inwards.

The most important mental drivers of this aspect are the eyes; they define the decisiveness implied by the word *kime*. If they are not looking strongly into the target, the focus will diverge, and the power will dissipate. Much of the concentration in focus can be tied into the direction of gaze (where the eyes are pointed) during the attack. If they point at the floor, that is where the power will go, and the body will tend to hunch over. If they are off center, the technique will slide off target, and so forth. The eyes themselves must point at the horizon to keep the body axis stable, but the attention can be placed freely wherever in the visual field it is needed so as to see the entire opponent.

A good method of practicing the feeling of looking and focusing outwards is with bicycle innertubes. As mentioned in the previous section on stance and stepping, have the students each find about five, 26-inch innertubes, and link them together into a long elastic rope (without cutting the loops, but removing the valve stems). Attach this elastic rope to some strong support below hip level and train by (1) walking out to the length of the tires with the hand holding the tires hanging behind, then (2) doing counterpunches so that the impact focus is held for about one second after the punch while keeping the eyes looking strongly at one point on the horizon. The exercise can be made more challenging by increasing the tension in the innertubes with more distance from the anchor point. After about 100 punches, the arm is sufficiently tired that the punch must be performed by whipping the hip around to generate force, and the body muscles must cooperate in the focus to prevent the arm and waist from buckling under the pull of the innertubes. If the eyes drop, both power and the individual's *will* can suffer. To produce the same effect for blocks (good linkage with focus), practice the first *Heian kata* with light weights in the hands. The torque on the shoulder cuff muscles will enforce connection and focus. As usual, beware of excess power and speed applied too early. In this case, it can do actual damage to both the shoulder and elbow joints.

To improve the speed aspects of a focus, i.e., attaining a high terminal velocity with sudden stopping of the fist, one of the better methods is punching at a candle flame. Set up a candle at a convenient height and distance, and punch at the flame with a locked-out counterpunch (not a snap). The fist is the piston that pushes a wall of air at the candle flame. If, with a punch stopping one inch away from the flame, the candle goes out, the focus is good. When this becomes easy, set up two candles in a row, one about one and one-half inches behind the other. First attempt to extinguish both flames, then only the back flame with the punch. This will only happen when the punch makes the air flow in a smooth fashion, and the turbulence formed by the punch begins about two inches away from the fist's surface at its final position.

Another method to help the connection of the fist to the body is to practice carrying books, briefcases, and other objects with only the ring and little fingers of the hand.

Finally, before doing any of the special punching drills, practice feeling the heartbeat in the fingertips for a minute or so. This will produce a feeling that the fingers are actually getting fatter and will move the mental focus from being internally directed towards projection of *ki* (see Chapter 9).

Chapter 5
Thrusting and Striking

Many techniques practiced by beginning students seem to lack definition and clarity, especially some of the kicking techniques like side snap kick and side thrust kick. Part of this problem in technique comes from an excess of concentration on the actual part contacting the target (hand or foot shape) rather than on the power flow into the target and the concomitant balancing of power through the pull back side.

Separation of the concepts of thrust and strike, both with the hands and the feet, is essential.

Additionally, the concepts of lockout and snapback techniques must be separately considered, as these terms form another dimension independent from and orthogonal to the thrust and strike concepts.

To expand on the idea of the "orthogonality" of technique classifications, it helps to think of a geometric analogy, and remember using graph paper in school to plot points and lines in 2-dimensional space (the page). If I draw a horizontal line (the x-axis) and put "strike" on one end and "thrust" on the other, the implication is that there might be techniques partway in-between that are part thrust and part strike. An example might be a punch that starts out as a strike, which can happen if the fist is not in a convenient place at the start of the technique. Likewise, I can draw a vertical line that intersects this x-axis in the middle and put the words" lockout" and "snapback" at opposite ends of this y-axis. Again, we imply that one can have techniques that have characteristics of both lockout and of snapback, such as some short snapping punches that do not return to their initiation point. In this way, the graph paper has defined a plane measured by the 2 orthogonal (90 degrees apart) axes, and on which any hybrid technique can be placed.

Now, for initial training, hybrid techniques will only confuse the student. First the endpoints of these axes must be clearly learned and be easily demonstrated before the student should begin to consider intermediate forms. Simply put, first learn to do the four clear corners of the graphed technique space: A lockout punch, a snapback punch, a lockout strike and a snapback strike.

5.1 Definition

One easy way to clarify the difference between a thrust and a strike is to simplify the limb and consider only the last long bone—the shin or forearm.

A thrust will generate force into a target and will move the target away from the limb in the direct line that this long bone is pointing. For example, a straight punch will push the target directly away, as will a side-thrust kick.

In contrast to a thrust, a strike will propel the target 90 degrees away from the direction this long bone points. For example, a hammer fist will drive the target in the direction pointed to by the bottom of the fist (as if one held a spike in the fist). This applies also to the feet in, for example, a pure front snap kick, which rises into the target and seems to lift it off the floor.

Another way of saying this is by analogy: Thrusts approach their targets in the same manner as spears or arrows; strikes approach their targets as do clubs or axes.

Occasionally, strikes have been called circular as opposed to linear techniques. This is not quite accurate; a better word to define this might be "angular," i.e., a linear technique approaching from a rotated position. Truly circular techniques tend to move their targets tangentially rather than penetrating them. Both thrusts and strikes ideally contact their targets at 90 degrees (perpendicular) and penetrate them. Circular techniques approach their targets at acute angles to invest them with motion, e.g., a parry that turns into a throwing technique.

5.2 Trajectories

The differentiation between lockout and snapback techniques is also relatively simple, but often gets confused with the strike and thrust concepts. This is because front snap kicks (for example) are usually done as strike-snapback techniques while punches are done as thrust-lockout techniques. That the opposite pairings in these techniques are possible and in fact useful is seldom considered for basic training in traditional karate (although the advanced forms do catalog them).

A simple example is the backfist strike. As a snapback technique, the hand is whipped out generally with a reverse hip rotation and snapped at the target with the focus completing at the end of the recoil, that is, unweighted. As a lockout technique, the hand is still whipped at the target, but the weight follows (usually with a direct rotation hip) and sinks into it, with the focus firming the elbow and arm at impact.

The same pairing can occur with punches: The thrust can either be locked out as a standard, hard, straight punch, or it can be snapped back like a boxer's short, straight jab.

Thus, the difference between side snap kick (a strike-snapback technique) and side thrust kick (a thrust-lockout technique) becomes easy to understand. One of the two other intermediate kicks, occasionally called a "mule kick," is a side thrust-snapback kick. An application of the reversed combination, a side snap kick using a locked (albeit slightly bent) knee joint, can be found in judo's **hane-goshi** (springing hip) throw, which appears to have a side snap-type of leg position applied to the inner aspect of the opponent's leg and ends with the leg lift stopping in the air without a snap-back movement.

The front snap kick also can be practiced as a mixed form kick, with the basic snap component augmented by a strong hip push into the target, producing a thrusting trajectory at the end.

An image that may help separate the feelings is that snapback techniques attempt to impart a vibration to the target, while lockout techniques attempt to go through it. Visualize a drum and drumstick: The best tone (vibration) is produced when the stick bounces with no extra weight behind it, but the drum head can be broken through if the stick is forced dagger-like into the drum head. Hard mobile targets are normally attacked with snapping strike techniques (e.g., the head), and softer, relatively immobile targets with lockout thrust techniques (e.g., the torso).

All linear techniques delivered with the distal points of the limbs can be classified as either thrusts or strikes, and simultaneously as either lockout or snapback.

It needs to be emphasized that these techniques are defined by their trajectories, and not by their endpoints. As such, it is important that techniques be considered as "verbs" and not as "nouns", even though the common labels are nouns, e.g. down block, front punch, etc. In actuality, the student is "blocking downward" or "punching towards the front," that is moving a limb through space and time, and not simply attaining an end-position. If, for instance, an arm that is performing an "up block" circles laterally to its final position, the face is never actually swept free of an incoming attack, and the "block" fails of its effect, even though the end position may be correct. An instructor should spend more time correcting the course of the techniques, and far less time worrying about the details of the end position. Karate is a movement discipline; correction solely of static postures will not allow a student to progress.

CLASSIFICATION OF LINEAR TECHNIQUES

	SNAPBACK	LOCKOUT
THRUST	LINEAR UN-WEIGHTED	LINEAR WEIGHTED
STRIKE	ANGULAR UN-WEIGHTED	ANGULAR WEIGHTED

EXAMPLES	VIBRATION SNAPPING PUNCH	STEPPING STRAIGHT PUNCH
	REV. ROTATION BACK-FIST STRIKE	DIRECT ROTAT. BOTTOM-FIST HAMMER STRIKE

**Figure 5
Linear Techniques**

Lockout techniques generally have the body weight moving into them via direct rotation or translation; snapback techniques derive their impact primarily from speed by reverse rotation or hip vibration. The opposite pairings are also possible.

One final note on elbows and knees as well as centrifugal kicks: Elbow and knee attacks are, by definition, lockout techniques (no joint to bounce back with), although they can be either strikes or thrusts. Centrifugal kicks as practiced by many Korean styles are generally locked out, but pass through the target as strikes (spinning heel), and occasionally as thrusts (bent knee spinning side and back kicks). Snapping versions of the hook or heel kick also can be done, generally with a shuffle side step and a reverse crescent kick trajectory.

What always must be kept clear is 1) the state of the knee or elbow joint at the completion of the focus—locked into position or snapped back, and 2) the connection between the striking surface and the target—in-line or angled.

With these differentiations in mind, smooth and clearly defined techniques can be performed. Admittedly, ideal combinations may not be possible depending on circumstances, but in basic practice, clear link-age and definition are essential.

5.3 Impact & Focus

If "focus" is thought of merely as muscular tension, the danger exists that techniques will be performed incorrectly with "dynamic tension." That is, the arm in a punch will have the antagonistic muscles slowing the limb extension long before impact, resulting in a "pushed" rather than a "thrown" punch. The effect on impact can be seen by graphing speed versus time (see Figure 6).

Using the arm muscles too early may provide a faster initial arm movement, but will slow the arm down as it reaches its full extension, thus producing a parabolic curve in time. On the other hand, throwing the punch with the hip movement leading the arm extension will produce a more peaked curve with the maximum speed occurring closer to the impact point.

In order to do this, visualize the fist attached to the arm as a rock on a string, that is, the upper arm and elbow joint are soft but the fist is strongly clenched. Think of the hips as a whirling platter with the rock attached by chewing gum to the rim. At peak hip speed, the gum gives way and the fist flies off at the 90 degree tangent direction as it takes the momentum of the hip. The focus is delayed as long as possible without hyper-extending the elbow. The final deceleration (change of speed per unit of time) is a measure of the impact focus of the technique.

Speed of "Pushed" versus "Thrown" techniques

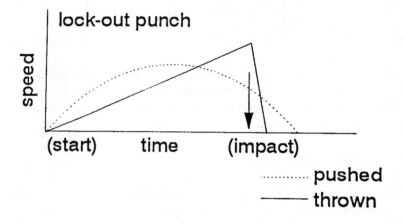

Figure 6
Pushed vs. Thrown

Graph of approximate speed vs. time during the travel of a lockout punch, both pushed (dotted line) and thrown or whipped (solid line) at a target. The pushed punch is faster earlier, but the thrown punch has a higher final velocity at impact.

Damage Potential vs Impact Distance

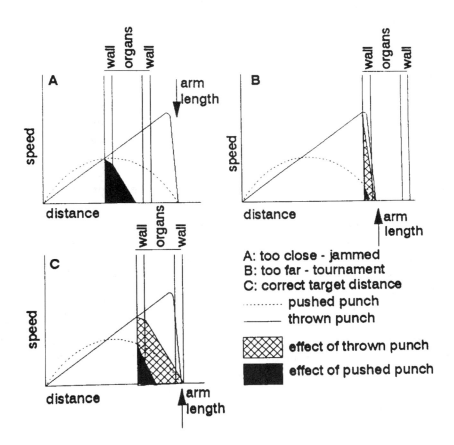

**Figure 7
Damage vs. Distance**

Graph of speed vs. distance of the same lockout punch showing impact at three different places: (A) too close, and therefore jammed; (B) too far, as is common in tournament techniques; and (C) correct, with maximum energy transferred to the target. The ideal target aiming point therefore is the back body wall for maximum shock to the internal structures. In all but the close in target, the thrown technique will generate more impact.

In figure 7, the shaded areas under the triangular power curves correlate to the energy that will be dissipated into the target as it is hit. So it can be seen that very short punches will have greater destructive potential when they are simply locked to the body and the body as a whole is launched at the target. As the punching range approaches the optimal distance, the thrown punch gains a greater impact than the pushed punch.

Training for this type of punching again is best done by candle punching. Also, bag punching with the idea of sharply folding, rather than pushing, the bag is helpful. The sound the bag makes upon impact will indicate the final velocity of the technique: The higher the note, the faster was the punch and the sharper was the impact.

In other words, have students try to create a "smack," rather than a "thud" upon impact and their focus will correspondingly improve with the improving arm relaxation during the flight of the fist.

Punching post *(makiwara)* training also will help (good auditory feedback) and, in addition, by aiming some three to six inches through the pad, and then holding the board flexed after impact, the stance and body lock components of focus are emphasized. Alternatively, if the speed elements are to be emphasized, strike the *makiwara* as hard and swiftly as possible, but allow the board to spring back freely with the goal of inducing a maximum transient deflection into the board. Avoid, however, the error of going too far through the *makiwara*—this leads to off-balance leaning and bad habits that will haunt the student in free sparring applications.

5.4 Targeting

The damage produced in each part of a target (e.g., a cubic inch) depends on the energy absorbed by that piece per unit of time. From this one fact proceeds the rationale for high terminal velocity techniques hitting at a peak speed as late in their flight as possible and supported by as much body mass as possible. The compromises that are made with this rationale are forced essentially by the need for balance and recovery during and between techniques, and will, as a result, diminish the effectiveness of the individual technique. Coupling the energy into the target efficiently brings into play other factors, of course, including the shape, hardness or softness of both the anatomical weapon and the impact site as well as angle of impact, and so on. But with all other factors being held constant, hitting faster and having a shorter focus to the technique will produce greater effect. This may seem obvious, but explicitly emphasizing this helps prevent the tendency to play "tag" during sparring practice in favor of "real" techniques.

To give specific examples is easy: A beginning sparring student often will push an arm out toward an opponent in an attempt to forestall or abort an incoming attack sequence in the hope that such a movement will be interpreted as a counter attack. While such a technique may actually land, it is ineffective because it has neither focus nor body commitment behind it.

Alternatively, the student may charge and, in the absence of a corresponding retreat by the opponent, simply end up pushing rather than striking the intended target.

Corresponding with these errors are errors in distancing, since the two aspects of targeting (when and where) interact: To make time, one must build distance from the opponent, and to make distance, one must move faster than the opponent. The distance factor can go in both directions—both closer and farther from the opponent. This is the concept labeled *ma-ai:* usually translated as "distance" in normal speech, but actually implying a larger concept of "interval" (see Chapter 11, Sparring). For now, suffice it to say that there is an appropriate interval that depends on the relationship between the positions, movements, reaction time and speed of the partners in which a technique can be effective.

It is common experience in free sparring to be able to "smother" or jam up an opponent's technique so that even if one is struck, no significant damage can result since the punch is still too early in its flight to build significant speed. The converse is also true—one can "fade" in front of a technique, leaving it over-extended and again powerless to inflict damage. If one graphs speed versus distance (rather than time—see again figure 7), one can see that there is an optimal targeting distance (and thus time required to perform it) for every technique at which it will produce the greatest amount of impact, even if the technique itself is flawless.

Students tend to try to make up distance by overextending an attack, rather than by moving the body closer. With emphasis on the idea that the student's arm cannot be lengthened, basic sparring practice should focus on positioning the body for optimal counterattack. This distance will be set by one's body proportions, and is one of the points that two opponents of different sizes vie for: the smaller person will want to be inside the effective distance of the taller one. However, the smaller person must cross the taller opponent's most dangerous distance first to get there, and then must be able to stay there until the job is done.

Conversely, the taller person will want to crush the smaller person from a distance with long-range attacks. How one initiates and handles such attacks is the definition of tactics, and depends not only on timing and sensing, but even more importantly on the will to attack. Just seeing an opening is not enough; it must be acted on.

Beyond the aspects of penetration depth and power delivery is the question of exactly where to hit, i.e., the local vulnerability of the opponent's body. In many karate books, there are listings and illustrations of so-called vital points at which the effect of a strike is claimed to be much more powerful than at neighboring areas. Obvious examples from boxing include the solar plexus and the point of the chin. Others usually listed are over the kidneys, on the neck (both sides, back, and throat), on the floating ribs, in the groin, and at the temples. Even more points have been extracted from acupuncture texts and can include claims of delayed or cumulative effects.

Additionally, places where major nerves cross edges of long bones and are available for attack have been included, the radial nerve in the forearm near the wrist being probably the most commonly known. A good illustrated anatomy text is crucial to an exploration of such vulnerabilities. Explicitly learning these points is useful and, provided that one is given the chance to target them precisely, the self-defense techniques themselves become more reliable in their effect. Whether this chance is an actuality in such situations can be questionable.

Further, such targeting should not be used in the sport applications of karate (*kumite*, free sparring) simply because of the safety implications, nor are they necessary for *kihon* practice. However, they can influence the self-defense interpretations *(bunkai)* of *kata* movements and should be separately explored.

Chapter 6
Kicking

Compared to the eight-, six-, and four-legged creatures that co-inhabit this planet with us, the human two-legged stance is an accident in balance waiting to happen. Add to this the proposal that we should pick one of these legs up and use it to transmit impact force into a target strains credulity.

Nevertheless, certain methods of training do build stability. One of these is a somewhat artificial differentiation between kicks. In fact, some styles boast of the number of different kicks they teach their students. This obscures and confuses the difference between training and application.

As with stances, kicks form a continuum of leg extensions. For example, start with an inside roundhouse kick, then continue without setting the foot down to use the same leg to do a front kick, then a half round kick, an outside crescent kick, a roundhouse kick, a side snap kick, a side thrust kick, a rising heel kick, a snapping hook kick, a back kick, and finally a snapping back kick. Throughout the sequence of kicks, all that is really changing is the degree to which the hip has been turned and the attack angle of the foot. The hip can be turned in the other direction while using the same foot and all the kicks sent off as their "spinning" variations, doing the above sequence in reverse order.

So it could be said that there is only one kick; all other named kicks are only variations separated for the convenience of teaching. In fact, both the front kick and the side kick are often made into hybrid kicks, with both circular and linear components, rather than being executed in their pure form. The pure form of the front snap (*mae-keage* or front-up) kick would have as its possible targets only areas such as the groin and the underside of the chin, exactly as the side snap (*yoko-keage* or side-up) kick. These rising kicks usually have been practiced with snap-back dynamics and are referred to as "snap kicks," while the thrust versions have been practiced with lock-out dynamics. The hybrid forms start as a rising kick, finish with the thrusting trajectory, but use the snap-back dynamics.

One way to make clear the differences between the pure forms of these kicks is to tie them into the same methods of power generation noted in the initial chapter on the movement of the body center.

The forward and back directions correspond to front and back thrust kicks. The side to side directions correspond to side thrust kick; there is no thrust to the opposite side since that would pass through the stance leg. Up and down vectors correspond to stamping kicks for the downward direction; the upward direction is again impossible due to the human body construction. The rotational modes around these prime directions imply the snapping variations of the kicks.

These kick sets are fully paired sets since the rotation occurs with the action of the knee. The front snap kick to the chin is the forward member of a pair with the back snap kick to the groin. The side snap kick pairs with the returning wave kick seen in the *Tekki kata*. The roundhouse snap kick pairs with the heel or hook kick.

Alternatively, one can think of the basic five kicks (front, side, round, hook, and back) as having both snapping (striking) and thrusting (penetrating) variants.

This classification scheme places more emphasis on the trajectories of the knee and foot than on the method of power generation.

Finally, at least some kicks can be linked to muscle tensions made in the various stances. For a specific example, the side snap kick at impact feels and is shaped something like a side stance but with one of the feet in the target; the side thrust kick is like a half-front facing stance while looking backwards over the rear shoulder and with the rear foot placed into the target.

These points need to be dealt with in teaching kicking, but probably in separate class sessions so as not to confuse the student with too many concepts at once.

6.1 Leg Extension

For maximum power, the kicking leg must be folded initially as tightly as possible under the thigh, the knee quickly lifted and pointed at the target prior to the actual extension of the leg, i.e., during the initiation phase. Lifting too high will slow the kick and telegraph the intent; lifting too low will jam the toes into the opponent's shin or knee. At the moment of focus of the kick, not only must the kicking leg be stretched, but so too must the support leg be stretched, so that as far as possible, all corners between the floor under the support leg and the target are minimized, provided of course that balance and recoverability are maintained (see fig. 8).

FRONT KICK AT FOCUS/IMPACT

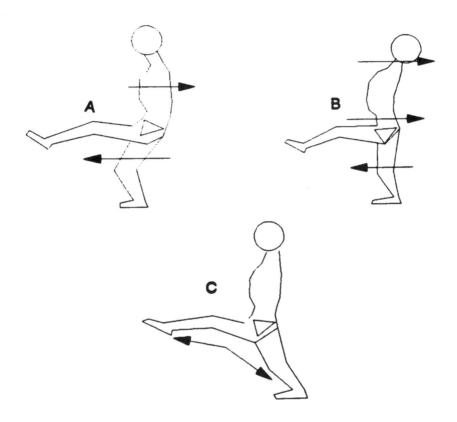

**Figure 8
Front Kick**

A: too much stomach tension at impact producing a rounding of the back and a collapsing of the stomach muscles (hollowness);
B: too much back tension causing a lean back (rearing);
C: balanced tensions allowing a smooth coupling of the floor to the technique with both legs feeling stretched.

Of course, one corner cannot be removed—that between the legs. To some extent this is compensated for by the weight of the upper body riding on top of the hips; nevertheless, the feeling of stretching both legs is critical. If some inequality between the legs should remain, it should be biased toward stretching the support leg more than the kicking leg (e.g., step long but kick short). This emphasis on the driving leg will help prevent an opponent from easily blocking the leg and using that block to unbalance the attacker.

In side thrust kick, for example, it is easy to let the upper body lean over and not to turn the hip over in-line with the kick, that is, to let the hips project backwards. Thus, in side thrust kick there are three arches that should be felt: One between the heels and legs from the floor to the target; one along the back to the kicking leg to keep the body in line with the thrust vector; and one between the leading shoulder and the leg, connecting the armpit and the hip and buttock while stabilizing the spine into essentially a neutral position (see figure 9). Further, the feeling should be that the lower (supporting leg) hip joint is actually moving toward the target, while avoiding excessive lateral curvature of the spine. The support foot must also turn for both the side thrust kick and the roundhouse kick so that there is no twisting action on the knee joint itself.

Control of the final impact position can be helped by twisting the pullback hand on the kicking leg side outwards (palm-up and rotating in the direction of the thumb side).

An excellent way to practice this kicking stretch is, again, with bicycle tire innertubes. Anchor the tubes close to the ground, and loop the tube around the ankle. Add a twist to the innertube, and hold the smaller loop between the big and second toes, then walk out to the length of the tubes before setting up the initial stance. Front kicks from front stance can be practiced efficiently this way, but other kicks such as side snap and side thrust from a twist stance, and back kick from front stance also will benefit.

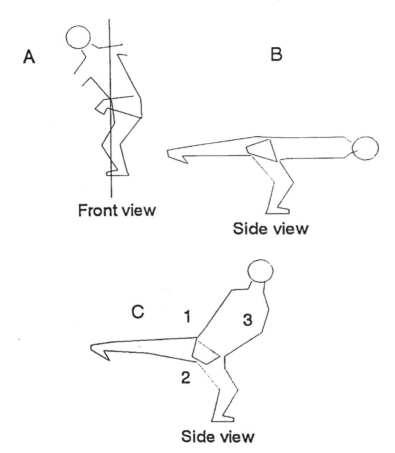

**Figure 9
Side Thrust Kick**

A: front view of kick at impact with too much stomach tension illustrating hip projection to the side and the compensating body lean, both at 90 degrees to the kick;

B: excess back tension without compensation resulting in body lean away from the target (side view).

C: side view showing the three arches of tension needed to focus at impact: 1- shoulder to hip, 2- stretch between legs, 3- back shoulder to buttocks rotating hip over.

6.2 Sweeps And Blocks

Foot sweeps are really only an application of a striking type of kick that attacks a stance leg on a vector that is parallel to its weak direction.

For instance, place an opponent in a left foot forward front stance facing you, and consider that you are facing 12:00 o'clock. The line connecting the opponent's feet runs parallel to the 4:00 to 10:00 line; the weak angle is 90 degrees away, or parallel to the 8:00 to 2:00 line. The simplest sweep is with one's own right foot striking from the outside of the opponent's stance to move their front foot toward and hopefully across their centerline, and thus onto their weak angle. These angles are really the "failure modes" of the stance—feet normally slip sideways and forwards, rarely backwards. Sweeps merely enhance this slippage in the most efficient manner available.

The path the sweep moves along should be an arc whose center is the opponent's body center. This ensures that the sweep will not only affect the leg, but also spin the opponent off balance by moving their hips. If the sweep track is straight or an arc that pulls the foot away from the body center, the sweep may topple the opponent, but it will not spin them effectively. The track chosen depends on what reaction the sweeper needs from the opponent to facilitate the concomitant attack.

More specifically, an opponent's stance foot can be attacked two ways: By sweeps or by reaps. Sweeps are essentially crescent kicks at floor level comparable to judo's *kosotogari* and *kouchigari*. As in judo, the position of the support foot is critical: It must be placed so that it not only points at the opponent's centerline, but also so that at impact, the sweeper's feet are about shoulder width apart, rather than in front of one another. Reaps are floor level hook kicks similar to *osotogari* and *ouchigari*. These reaps can be done either spinning or with a shuffle step (judo commonly uses the shuffle step). In either case, the attack can only succeed when the opponent's attention is drawn upward so as to "unroot" the stance (at least psychologically) before the sweep or reap hits. Further, the upper body must to some extent be immobilized, usually by controlling one of the opponent's arms.

The sweep itself is not an attack in and of itself; it is only an opening move intended to permit the real attack (a follow up punch, kick, or strike) to be delivered successfully and with maximum effect. Practice of sweeps must include the finishing technique to prevent students from freezing at the moment of a successful sweep, thus losing the opening they have created.

Another application of kicking is blocking. Leg blocks can be either deflections, such as crescent kicks with the foot, shin, or knee, or interceptive "stop thrusts," either to the body or to the attacking limb itself. Timing in these techniques is critical, and while use of them can be effective, they tend to prevent effective continuation of the counterattack due to increased distance from the opponent. Their principles of movement are the same as the equivalent arm techniques, with the important difference that balance is more easily upset and the block itself more easily countered.

Chapter 7
Blocking

When faced with an attack, the instinctive reaction is to attempt to interpose the hands while flinching away. With beginning sparring students (about one year of training), defense is usually accomplished much the same way by receiving the attack on an arm or leg placed in front of the perceived target. Later, with practice, the student tries to hit the side of the attacking limb (at an angle of 90 degrees to the limb) with a "power block," thus deflecting the force of the attack rather than absorbing its direct impact. This method prevents serious damage, but can produce deep bruises on the arm and/or leg bones in both partners.

It is at this method of hard blocking combined with the need to withdraw from the attack where many students may get stuck in their training. In fact, some dojos are known for encouraging this "baptism of pain" as a sort of initiation into acceptance by the higher ranked students. Such students do not get beyond the requirement to explicitly wind up and strike an attacking arm or leg while simultaneously retreating from the opponent. This then leads to the situation in free sparring in which the two opponents launch single attacks at each other, block while retreating to the point that the block was actually unneeded, and then may be too far away or too slow to counterattack.

Beating the forearms and shins with baseball bats can desensitize them to impact, but such practices cannot be healthful and have been known to induce phlebitis (the accumulation of blood clots in the extremities).

If trained in this manner, even when the student learns to parry, the same mentality generally prevails (to strike the attack away, often during a retreat), and the counterattack is slower than could be accomplished with a different understanding of blocking.

7.1 Definition

The problem with blocking is that it is mentally perceived as a push. That is, it automatically generates the assumption that distance will be increased between the opponent and oneself. Additionally, no differentiation is made in the term "blocking" between what is functionally a simultaneous counterattack on the opponent's punching or kicking limb and a technique that exists to unbalance the opponent so as to permit a follow-up counter. More to the point, the Japanese term *uke* actually translates to "reception" rather than blocking/parrying. This implies a completely different attitude toward dealing with an attack, that of taking the attack as a tool rather than repelling it.

A "block," rigorously defined, is just that, a blockade of an entry vector. It is passive. The analogy of a rock blocking the entrance to a cave is perfectly correct and illuminating. There are no such techniques in competent karate in my opinion. In common parlance, block is used generically rather than specifically, and includes any and all defensive actions involving contact between some portion of the defender's anatomy with some portion of the opponent's, and might also include tactical blocking (closing off lines of attack by positioning alone). However, the fact that the term "block" has been used by default for all *uke-waza* makes it no more useful in describing what's going on, and as misleading as phlogiston was in describing what went on with fire, or the four humors for describing real physiology in ancient medicine. I do not advocate passive interposition of any portion of a defender's anatomy in direct opposition to the attack vector of any opponent's technique. By this definition, one should not "block" – one should parry, trap, redirect, evade, or counterstrike the attacking limb. In fact, it may be possible that the use of the term "block" can foster a purely reactive mindset, making the more advanced interceptive counters more difficult to learn than they need be. For the purposes of consistency with the existing literature, I will reluctantly use the term "block" but with the implied understanding that it remains merely shorthand for the real techniques involved.

While attacking the opponent's thrust is a viable technique (some Okinawan styles have no other form of blocking), it should not be labeled a block by strict definition, but rather a counter-strike to the attacking limb. True blocking actually should be a kind of a pull that permits the blocker to evade the attack while the attacker feels the attack falling into a vacuum where there was once a target.

The actual blocking of an attack requires two elements: The matching of velocities and the blending and redirection of the attack before its focus. This concept occasionally has been labeled soft or circular blocking as opposed to hard or linear blocking. Aikido insists on this circular method of accepting an attack in order to control it, both because it is more efficient (less strength required) as well as because it permits a more controlled interaction, i.e., one can defend without necessarily damaging the opponent.

Specifically, the difference can be seen in the outside block: the hard, linear block smashes into the attacking forearm at 90 degrees with the intent to break it; the soft circular block reaches out to the arm early in a comma-shaped trajectory and rides it in while applying only sufficient pressure to steer it out of the target area and extend it beyond where it had originally been intended to stop. Further, this soft blocking actually attempts to take functional possession of the attacking limb, and through it, control the attacker's balance and posture. The same difference can be applied to the other blocks as well. Some of the advanced blocks (hooking, scooping, and so on) must be done circularly, or they will not work at all.

7.2 Classification

Circular techniques in general can be classified like the strokes of a sword blade. Circular strokes can be distinguished from the linear attack modes of thrust (poke) and strike (chop). Actual use will cross or combine these classes, but for teaching purposes, there are two blade positions and two blade movement directions in respect to the target, which in this case, is the limb (see figure 10).

In circular use, the sword blade either can pull in or push out (extend); in position, the blade can be oriented either across the attacking limb, or in-line (parallel) with it. Thus an in-line pull is a slashing motion such as a hooking block or reaping throw; a cross-line push is a planing action such as a pushing foot-sweep.

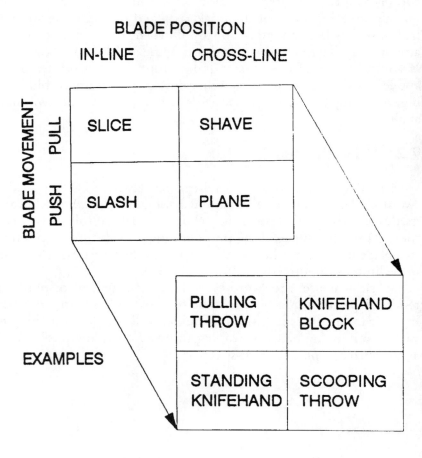

Figure 10
Circular Techniques

The tracks of all circular techniques are segments of circular arcs and contact their targets on the tangent. Push and pull are defined in relation to the body center. Examples are general only. The techniques cited can also cross into other classes in actual application. See text for further examples.

To demonstrate this differentiation, get a wooden sword *(bokken)* and find a heavy hanging bag. The first technique is the thrust—a poke with the tip. The second technique is the chop with the cutting edge, which will move the bag laterally. These are the only two possible linear attacks. Now place the sword edge horizontally on the side of the bag. Pushing the blade forward away from the body center while exerting side pressure is a slice; pulling the blade towards one's body center with the same side pressure can be called a slash. These techniques tend to rotate the bag. The slice, especially, can be done with the blade reversed, i.e., with the hands leading and the blade laid back along the arm while the hands extend away from the body center.

The cross-line techniques can be demonstrated against a horizontal staff while holding the sword vertically. The staff can be shaved either with a pull or a push (sword blade can be held either up in the normal orientation or down as if it were a dagger).

For the sword, the concept of blade placement is critical; for the hand, it is less so. The in-line and cross-line positions are better reflected in the elbow position for empty hand techniques: In-line techniques will have the forearm and elbow lined up relatively parallel to the attack vector, while cross-line techniques will have the elbow bent and generally dropped so that the arm crosses the attacking limb.

Equivalent hand techniques that can be visualized include, for example, the bent elbow knife hand block as a cross-line pull; the standing knife hand used in a charge as an in-line push; the pull used on a punch to make a throw as an in-line pull; the movement used to scoop a kick and dump the opponent backwards as a cross-line push. These techniques are not completely independent—if the opponent's technique has much drive, in-line can become cross-line. If the opponent resists the pull or push, the force can be swung around into its complement for effectiveness.

Most individual circular techniques can be modified to work in both in-line and cross-line shapes, and with either the pull or the push as the driving force. As with all these concepts, these techniques must be visualized clearly and practiced repeatedly before they can be applied effectively.

7.3   Circular Shifting

Blocking is closely related to shifting, and especially to circular shifting in which the defender's feet cross behind each other during the turning movement. Consider the following technique: The attack is a right stepping punch to the stomach; the defender is in natural stance. The block to be used is a left arm outside block. Have the attack occur slowly enough so that the block can be set up and moved to the point of contact between the arms before any defensive body shifting occurs, generally at the point that the attacker's feet are beside each other. Then, and only then, have the defender start to move the right foot behind the left as the hips rotate clockwise. The feeling to be taught is that the advancing attack actually pushes on the defender's hips via the arm connection, rotating them out of the way of the attack. The shift and block complete with the defender oriented across the line of the attack and giving pressure to the outside of the attacking arm. Be very careful that the separation between the partners remains "real" so that the endpoint of the attack technique would, in the absence of the reception, actually have successfully struck its target. Otherwise, the exercise reverts to meaninglessness, since the block would not actually have been required.

The important concept to be grasped here is not the fact that the attack can be used to power the defense, but that for the defense to be effective, the defender must also give weight and push into the point of contact, make it the center of the mutual movement, and then take control of that center. The attacker will be unbalanced by being forced to move on the periphery of the circle whose center is controlled by the defender. This unbalancing *(kuzushi)* is the hallmark of circular blocking.

A good way of practicing the feeling of this type of blocking using a cross-line pull circular mode (joining with the attack) while still shifting linearly is with "pendulum" training. This is a form of one-step basic sparring in which the partners alternate attack and defense roles.

The attacker starts in left foot forward front stance down block, the defender with right foot forward (knees almost touching—mirror stances, but with the attacker's foot offset so that it lands just inside the defender's anchor foot). The attacker steps forward with a front punch while the defender retreats one step with a block. On the next count the defender becomes the attacker and punches with a step forward, and the previous attacker steps back with the block.

After several tens of these back and forth movements, the block will get softer and the attack will get harder, i.e., the block will move earlier to ride instead of hitting the thrust, and the thrust will move faster with a stronger focus because the attacker will not fear the block's impact. Ideally, the block should make no sound upon touching the attacking arm, nor should the moving foot make a sound upon landing.

Next have the partners make 3, 5, 7 or 9 movements on one verbal count while increasing the speed of the movements. Initially, the emphasis should be on coordination, accuracy and especially full movements and accurate stance shifts, giving weight to both the attack and the block and rooting the anchor foot. Errors include rolling the edge of the anchor foot as well as the insertion of small cheat steps by the anchor foot on each shift. Later, an element of competition can be introduced in which the attacker attempts to drive the defender backwards during the attack so effectively that the defender cannot launch an attack strongly enough after the block to keep position, but this should be for brown belts and up. Timing and breathing become important factors as fatigue builds, and this exercise can be used to teach breath control in blocking.

Chapter 8
Linkage and Breath

The instructor must keep clear the understanding that a circular technique such as a parry or a block is not necessarily an "unfocused" technique. The difference sometimes is explained in the Chinese terms *yin* and *yang*. *Yin* and *yang* are Chinese words that label an essential philosophical duality in nature. Examples include for *yin* and *yang*, respectively, female and male, dark and light, wet and dry, weak and strong, and many others. Almost everything from foods to furniture to landscapes can be classified by the proportions of *yin* and *yang* they contain. In karate usage, a *yang* technique in general is performed on an exhalation and has its own focus. A *yin* technique, on the other hand, can be performed on either the inhale en route to another counter linked to it with the following out-breath (e.g., a sequential parry and counterpunch), or on an exhale, in which case it is actually sharing the exhalation with another technique that is the main focus of that breath (e.g., simultaneous parry and counterpunch). Most linear and angular blocks will be *yang*, while most circular blocks (or parries) will be *yin*. Locked out thrusts will tend to be *yang*, while *"en passant"* strikes will tend to be more *yin*.

Initially, beginners are taught to exhale strongly with each technique. Additionally, they are taught to force the breath with a voiced *kiai*, cutting the *kiai* off with a glottal stop in order to produce a strong, sharp, and short focus. In other words, the *kiai* must not trail off slowly and softly, but instead end sharply, coinciding with the sharp ending of the actual technique, as noted in the earlier chapter on breathing and focus. In this stage of practice, breathing in is limited to the setup motions. This ensures that the beginner learns to concentrate power into the techniques and to synchronize the contraction of the body muscles. Failure to understand that this is only the initial training method can lead to a stunted development of technique.

The results of exclusive use of this essentially *yang* method are twofold: 1) the inability to "let go" of a focus after it is completed, what is called "sticking" between techniques, and 2) *kata* that are staccato and metronome-like in execution even though they are strong in their individual techniques.

In *kumite*, the inability to continue to move and execute techniques on anything but an exhale results in, quite literally, "dead time" when one can be struck easily by an opponent.

It should seem logical that since we spend half of our life breathing in, half of our technique training should also be on the in-breath. The *tai chi chuan* classics state that while retracting the arm or extending the leg, breathe in; while extending the arm or retracting the leg, breathe out.

On the face of it, this seems contradictory to Western scientific thought; power is believed to flow from the out-breath. In both China and Japan, this is not so universally accepted.

Kyudo (Japanese Zen archery), for example, draws the bow on the in-breath, using the expansion feeling in the torso to push the hands apart, spreading the bow as opposed to simply drawing it. The initial entry and unbalancing of the opponent in *aikido* also tends to use the in-breath to lead out the opponent's *ki*, forcing them to overextend their out-breath.

So an initial impression useful for teaching is that pulling (or, more accurately, drawing out) can be done on the in-breath, but pushing must be done on the out-breath.

Once this concept is accepted and has been practiced in basic parry block-punch combinations, concentration on the pullback hand in technique will provide the required mental pulling motion to power the other hand's push on an in-breath.

To make this breath pattern work with techniques on a bag, the stomach muscles must be tensed outward so as to form a bulge, and the breathing action concentrated on the diaphragm. One can even perform punches on the in-breath, but their impact will feel very different from the normal, focused, out-breath punch. Such punches have applications in situations where a locked body is not required, such as a punch performed while flowing into a throwing position.

8.1   Kata Examples

Goju-ryu karate explicitly demonstrates the in-breath form of blocking in the *Sanchin kata*. One of the techniques in that *kata* involves turning 180 degrees while executing an inside block that occurs on the in-breath.

One example from the Shotokan *kata, Kanku Dai,* also shows the application of in-breath to attack techniques, although the technique is taught to most brown belts as a purely out-breath combination, as follows: In left front stance from a down block position, execute a right knife hand strike to the neck combined with a left hand rising knife hand parry, followed by a right front kick, that followed by a 180 degree turn counterclockwise to back stance with a left down block combined with a high right inside block to the (now) rear. If this is done with only out-breath focuses on each technique, the combination is very jerky (especially when the performer is tired) and the between technique in-breaths produce "dead time." Now, replace the out-breath on the kick with an in-breath, and the technique becomes smooth, swift, and flowing. The kick does not lose power, although the feeling of the snap kick changes. The combination continues with a second (segmented or stepped) out-breath focus on the palm heel thrust, and then an in- and out-breath pair for the draw back and "settling in" down block.

All the *kata* can be reconsidered from this point of view. For example, *Heian Shodan*, the first of the basic *Heian kata*, is normally taught with each technique separate and focused with an out-breath. Simply replace the out-breath of every block in the block-attack sequences with an in-breath, and the whole *kata* changes from a sequence of techniques to a sequence of combinations that have combat timing.

Lists of the other Shotokan *kata*, coded for breathing and linkages into sequences, are given in Appendix F.

With this understanding, another whole world of technique opens up—the world of *yin* techniques—in which the incoming power of an opponent is not opposed with the block, out-breath to out-breath, but rather welcomed into an apparent vacuum that pulls the opponent off balance forward and permits easy and almost effortless entry for counter-attack.

Finally, since the body's natural reaction to an unexpected startle or attack is an in-breath, it would make sense to use this reaction to generate the automatic block or deflection. For combinations, this implies a set of guidelines: In general, breathe in when blocking, breath out when attacking, and with sequential techniques, breathe alternately in and out. This is only a preliminary step in determining how to breathe in a combination; linking movements will include step-breathing as well to more closely combine focuses. Punching while breathing in produces a soft-focused and almost relaxed impact that feels very different from classical punching, but practice with the heavy bag will produce effectiveness even here.

The three types of breathing and their associated linkages have parallels to the medieval philosophical elements of which the world was nominally composed: The 4 exoteric physical elements of earth, air, fire, and water, and the esoteric, alchemical root element of spirit that underlies the others.

Miyamoto Musashi, the "Sword Saint" of Japan and author of *The Book of Five Rings*, speaks of such elements from a Buddhist perspective as well, providing images with which to identify while performing a particular technique or combination.

Earth would be quite strong and locked down into stance with strong, focused out-breaths and maximum penetration with impact.

Fire might follow the step-breath idea, with a quicker and sharper focus in tightly linked combinations, delivering greater shock to the target.

Water might include the in-breath shifting blocks with the following out-breath producing the countering technique, giving an ocean wave feeling to the movements, possibly including deflections and throws.

Air might include in-breath counters directly with shifts that avoid blocking entirely, such as angled stop-thrusts and shifts with back-fist strikes.

Spirit (the void, in Musashi's terminology) might refer to the mind that freely changes between all these feelings, without having to actively think or discursively select it, i.e., the mind following the shift in outlook and understanding of technique that occurs with the graduation from the *kyu* ranks (colored belts, ending usually at brown belt) to the *dan* ranks (the levels of black belt).

The in-breath concept does lead, however, to a problem in teaching beginning students how to lock down a focus, especially in *kata*. Here it pays to separate the learning into levels, and teach the five *Heian kata* as purely out-breath *kata* to those just beginning to learn. This makes *Heian Shodan* a *kata* with 22 in- and out-breaths.

Later, with the concept of *kata* as a set of combinations, block-attack links can be made and the in-breath limited to the preparation movements. This will drop the number of breaths to 15, using step-breaths on the three down block–stepping punch combinations, the hammer fist–stepping punch, the two final up blocks and two final stepping punches in the charges, leaving the remaining single techniques on their own in- and out-breath pairs. The final method using in-breath blocking will drop the total number of breaths to 10 (see the Appendix).

The ability to lock down the block, and thus be sure of its effectiveness, is not to be ignored in favor of the more advanced in-breath block. Only with the attainment of the *Tekki kata* (brown belt transition), the in-breath concept should begin to be practiced, and can be more fully expanded in the training in preparation for the *dan* rank.

With the black belt in hand, the first lesson is *Heian Shodan*, and the learning cycle begins again, but this time, the in-breath understanding coupled with the years of focus training will not compromise the effectiveness of the techniques.

8.2 Applications in Kata

The shift in emphasis in *kata* from a series of basic techniques to a series of self-defense combinations raises the need to understand exactly what it is that the techniques are doing with and to the visualized opponent.

Some teachers, especially in the more modern schools, view all *kata* simply as a catalog of formalized movements to be performed for historical purposes and ranking exams only. Others will emphasize to a greater or lesser extent the actual defense application (called *bunkai*) of the precise *kata* movements or the implied extension of some of these movements into techniques not actually in the *kata*. This expansion of techniques using the *kata* movement as a starting point is usually labeled *oyo*, and has been used to explain the apparently useless moves in the *kata*, i.e., those that do not appear to finish one opponent before moving on to the next.

However, there are neither useless moves nor moves that are purely setup moves in the traditional *kata*; if they appear so, the visualization of the opponent must be wrong.

A simple example occurs in *Tekki Shodan* at the movement following the first elbow strike.[1] This is a position (*koshi-gamae*) with the fists stacked over each other at the hip. This is usually explained as a setup position for the following down block only, i.e., there is no *bunkai* for this position. In a real fight, there is rarely time to set up—each movement must have some offensive capability in order to be viable. This should include the *yoi* movement (placing the hands over each other in front of the groin from their position in front of the thighs).

The exploration of *oyo* is a useful method of training, however. At the very least, the concept itself encourages the student into a fluidity of movement that prevents the techniques from ever running into a dead end from which the student cannot continue.

Further expansion of this idea are called *henka-waza* ("varied technique"), which build from the *oyo* to produce a much wider range of follow-up techniques.

---

[1] See: Schmeisser, E. T. Bunkai: Secrets of Karate Kata Vol 1: The Tekki Series. Tamashii Press, St. Louis, MO (2000)

To return the specific example above, from my understanding of Okinawan karate, there is much *ju-jutsu* in the art, i.e., many movements involve wrist locks, arm bars, and throws, rather than simply striking a standing opponent. A *bunkai* of the *yoi* of *Tekki* might be a parry with the right hand coupled with a left-hand ankle grab of a front kick attack from the right, done on the out-breath.

The next in-breath covers the cross-step and the knee kick into the bottom of the opponent's captured leg followed by the out-breath backhand attack to the head or neck. That hand remains open because it skips over the head and grabs it for the in-breath elbow attack to the pulled-in face.

The next move (*koshi-gamae*) is not a setup, but rather a pulling of the face down onto the hip (out-breath for power) to unbalance and further stun the opponent in preparation for the left arm, hair-pulling, cross-body, in-breath, yank of the opponent's head, opening the throat for the hook punch (out-breath).

In this series (techniques one through seven in the *kata* listing, comprising the first short sequence), there is not one wasted move, and each move is such that there are no openings in the self-defense. Each move is to be performed exactly as it is in the *kata*, i.e., the *bunkai* are complete without the necessity to invoke *oyo* to explain the *kata*.

Also note that the breath links pairs of techniques and sets the timing and syncopation of the form.

Elsewhere in the *kata*, there are positions with the fist under the elbow. Ostensibly, this position makes no sense, unless one visualizes that hand holding some part of the opponent's clothing or body.

The returning-wave kicks (techniques 12 and 14, *nami-gaeshi-geri*) in real practice probably cannot be groin deflection foot blocks (try it against a front kick, but gently). However, these movements easily can be attacks with the heel of the foot into the knee, inner thigh, or groin of a closely held opponent.

Another example of apparently useless movements comes from the opening movements of *Heian Yondan*.[2] If these and the following two movements (the cross block followed by the augmented block) are viewed from the *ju-jutsu* perspective, it can be seen that there is only one opponent directly in front, and that all four movements (techniques two through five, the first short sequence) are the setup and execution of a cross-twine throw, as in *aikido's juji-nage*.

---

[2] see: Schmeisser, E. T. Channan - The Heart of the Heians. Usagi Press Japan, Kanazawa, Japan (2004)

In *Chinte*, the final three movements (techniques 36–38 in the listings: a 45-degree hop with the hands coming to a palm over fist position in front of the chest, followed by two hops directly back to the *embusen*, or starting line) cannot be "hopping over bodies," as I was once told. Even if it is accepted that these hops were added purely to adjust the shape of the *kata* so that it ended where it began, an application can still be envisioned. Instead, the first move will work as an *aikido*-type of wrist lock (*nikyo*), using the grip and first hop to set the twist into the opponent's hand; the following two hops to force the opponent to the ground with a broken wrist.

In summary, all movements in *kata* must be linked, both by breathing and with each other into viable self-defense combinations.

In general, any time a hand is at the hip or in non-striking positions (e.g., under an elbow), it can be assumed to be holding some part of the opponent (body, limb, clothing, or weapon). Any time a hand appears to be simply making a set up or wind up motion, it can be assumed to be deflecting something or escaping a grip. Any time a movement appears useless, the attack or the target is being visualized wrongly.

It is a very useful practice to take each short sequence of each *kata* and place an attacker sequentially in each of the eight directions. From each of these directions, have the attacker attempt the three major types of attack with each hand (grab and punch, double hand grab, and kick) to whatever part of the defender is available. Then have the defender move through the short *kata* sequence exactly, watching carefully what happens to the opponent. The moves before and after the obvious short sequence also might be involved.

With this method of exhaustive exploration, at least one and often several *bunkai* can be discovered for each sequence. Each *kata* should be dissected and the combinations themselves practiced in class by the students on each other until they can express these applications with conviction in the performance of their *kata*. Then not only will the *kata* mean something to each individual, but also the lessons of breathing, stance, power, and linkage will be learned in the *kata* as something with real application, rather than simply elegant but empty movements or a fancy method to practice basic techniques.

Chapter 9
Timing

Timing can be taught in two realms—that relating to oneself and that relating to an opponent.

The first is the internal realm and is expressed in the relationships between individual movements in combination techniques.

The second is the external realm, which is a social one, dealing with the relationship between two or more individuals, and is expressed in the harmony (or clashing) of mutual movements in free sparring or actual fighting.

Good timing in both realms is a mark of self-mastery as well as of good technique, and thus is the goal towards which training is aimed.

9.1 Combinations

Timing in relation to one's own movements arises from the concept of centralized power generation and controls combination techniques. Essentially, techniques can only be combined, either in series (following each other) or in parallel (happening together), when their direction vectors are compatible. If the vectors are incompatible, the techniques must be separated by a focus before the combination can continue. This separation generates combinations that are staccato or show one-two timing, e.g., outside block–reverse punch. Compatible vectors produce timing in one count, e.g., simultaneous sliding parry-counterpunch. Vectors that are slightly separated in either space or time or both, but not opposed in direction, can produce one-and-a-half count ("and-one") timings, e.g., direct rotation knife-hand block followed by spear-hand thrust, or outside block followed by a lead (same) hand punch.

To repeat, the timings possible with executed techniques are three: **Simultaneous**, or in one; **sequential**, or in one-two; and finally **overlapping**, or in and-one. These timings refer to the movement of the limbs in relationship to the breath and focus, and can be practiced without an opponent.

In fact, all of these timings are cataloged in the *kata*. Serious study of the implied syncopation of the movements in *kata* combined with analysis of the breathing patterns and imaginary opponents will demonstrate that the "Three Cautions of *Kata*" (expansion and contraction of the body, light and heavy application of strength, and slowness and quickness in movement) are simply ways of practicing these timings in combinations. This is why classical *Karate-do*, which emphasized *kata* and *kata* applications to the exclusion of free sparring, still produced superb fighters.

From a training point of view and as mentioned before, it is most important that after the initial learning of the sequence of a *kata*, the form should be practiced as a set of combinations rather than a sequence of individual techniques. Thus the count during group practice should not occur at every technique (producing a metronome-like regularity), but with each short defense-counterattack sequence, producing a syncopated form matched to the idealized opponents' motions.

9.2 Opponents

The timings that refer to the temporal relationship between two opponents are, again, three: Pre-emptive (*sen-no-sen*), reactive (*go-no-sen*), and interceptive (*go-no-sen-no-sen*). The terms *tai-no-sen, tai-tai-no-sen,* and *sen-sen-no-sen* also are used by various teachers, and are placed into various sets that all deal with the same three basic ideas, namely **forestalling** (pre-emptive timing), **blending** with (simultaneous and interceptive timings), or **following** onto (reactive timing) the opponent's attacks, bearing in mind that any attack can be considered to start with an intention, rather than an overt movement. These timing concepts are common to kendo as well, and will be further explored in the chapter on sparring.

Pre-emption especially, therefore, can be split into at least two levels: Pre-empting the movement itself and pre-empting the prior intention, which usually is considered more difficult.

Nevertheless, there is a progression in ability that is reflected in timing, and should be pointed out when teaching.

Beginners usually are locked into reactive timing, and so use one-two types of combinations. Thus in sparring practice, it is almost impossible to induce them to attack. When attacked, they can block, but cannot counterattack in time. Also, their tempo of techniques in combination is very regular, and they succumb to fakes.

An analogy is of two meshing gears: Each tooth (attack) is matched by another (defense). The only way to win, therefore, is to somehow put two teeth together where only one would normally fit. Intermediate students can move into pre-emptive timing, and can make combinations with both simultaneous and one-two timings. Also, they have learned to insert fakes into the attack with the "and-one" timing. These students can get up their courage and charge in, often recklessly. The attack combinations are more syncopated, but their defenses are still single technique by single technique, and they rely on speed to counter both the opponent's defenses and attacks.

It is only those who have achieved the highest level who can consistently move with interceptive timing and overlapping techniques. Thus they appear to wait endlessly, but as soon as the attacker thinks to move, they are already moving; they blend with and take away the attack, countering before a second attack can be launched.

This is not due to superior speed. Again and again it is reported by onlookers that the master moved relatively slowly; only the attacker felt as if things occurred at blinding speed. Instead, the master matches velocities, leading in relative phase, rendering null the relative speed of the attacker's technique. Since both parties are now moving at the same speed, the relative velocity is zero and the master can use the mental time during the mutual movement to arrange the counter.

Essentially, the master is using the attack vector to spear the opponent with a fist apparently left there to be run into, pre-empting any second technique.

This, then, is true timing: The way to avoid the fight of strength against strength, not by superior speed, but by a softer responding that moves into and takes early control of the opponent's technique.

9.3 Ki

Speaking of the techniques and timing of Asian martial arts masters inevitably brings up the subject of *ki*. In the West, *ki* (alternatively *chi* or *qi*, translated variously as "breath power," "spirit force," "extension") may be considered a concept beyond effective verbal explanation and subject only to experiential knowledge: Either you have it or you don't; either you believe in it or not.

In Japan and China, the concept of *ki* has a longer history and generally is accepted, with applications in medicine as well as the martial arts. The flow of *ki* through the body is thought to determine health and illness. The issuing of *ki* is connected with effectiveness of technique in punching and kicking as well as throwing or unbalancing an opponent. Clouding the issue are apocryphal stories of masters blowing out candles from across the room by pointing a finger at them. These may be wonderful stories, but for the intermediate student, they are both baffling and irrelevant.

At the student level, the application of *ki* can be broken down most usefully into two teachable components—dynamic leverage and mental coordination *and* visualization. The concept of dynamic leverage includes that of static levers—using small forces on long arms to move heavy centers attached to them (e.g., any stance has at least one weak direction, any technique has at least one weak angle). Additionally, the concept includes the utilization of the forces produced by an attack in order to defeat it.

Examples include pulling on a moving punch just before its focus to more thoroughly upset an opponent than pushing it sideways or pulling at some other time; avoiding it to simultaneously counterattack into an oncoming body to multiply the impact. If, in addition, the counterattack is aimed into an anatomical weak point or nerve plexus, the perceived impact will be much greater than the physical one, all of which encourages the thought that some esoteric force (*ki*) was added to the technique that could not have been produced by the muscles. While this may be true, it does not help the student learn and can lead to an actual weakening of effort in the mistaken faith that *ki* will make up the difference.

The mental dimension of *ki* is the one that most often is taught—"extend your force to the horizon," or "flow with the movement," "...the opponent," or "...the technique" are the phrases used. This is used as a pedagogic trick designed to get the beginner's mind off of the physical details (in which the student tends to get swamped) and into the overall (and thus more coordinated) movement of a technique. Thus a punch done with *ki* has more power because the verbally thinking mind has gotten out of the way of the spinal and cerebellar feedback loops that have been trained past exhaustion into efficiency.

If the mind focuses on a detail (say, the hand twist), this will interfere with the smooth adding up of all the microforces from the muscle fibers in the coordinated and timed sequence necessary, and the situation develops in which each punch is worse than the preceding. The only way out is to stop and "let go" of the technique, i.e., extend the *ki*.

Combining dynamic leverage with the speed obtainable by relaxed, *ki*-filled punches produces good timing and optimal power generation.

9.4 Training

Interpersonal timing is normally developed in free sparring sessions. However, merely throwing a new student onto the floor to be pounded by some husky brown belt is only a way to eliminate those who most need and can benefit from the training.

Free sparring should be reserved until the student has at least a year of training in basics and kata so that technique will not completely fall apart under pressure and the student begin counterattacking in panic with wild and uncontrolled techniques. Proper training in sparring should allow the student to learn to move without excess tension, either mental or physical. Several exercises are useful for this.

Ten-step basic sparring at slowly increasing speeds (up to a run) forces not only accuracy, but coordination and the maintenance of proper distance between the partners. Also, basic one-step sparring, but with two possible targets—face or stomach—will force mental relaxation and the ability to wait effectively. Later, the attack can include a fake with both partners in more natural fighting stances, thus becoming "semi-free" sparring.

One level more difficult allows two or more possible attacks with two or more targets—step-in front kick or step-in front punch (either one) to either face or stomach—to be practiced. This method is an extremely important way of training, and is too often shortchanged in favor of full free sparring.

By taking turns, each individual is forced to learn how to make a committed attack in the face of a prepared opponent. By the use of the semi-free format, each individual is forced to learn how to respond quickly, position the defensive shift accurately, and counter attack strongly to prevent the attacker from escaping.

Next, in preparation for free sparring, attack combinations of up to four steps can be built, and a matching defense combination practiced, essentially the Chinese idea of two-man sets. Taking turns attacking in a free sparring format is also useful, partners executing their own "favorite combination" attack sequence while the defender attempts to defeat it. Slow motion sparring is one of the best, but most difficult training methods for timing, due to the temptation to cheat by speeding up the movements to compensate for a missed tempo. All these exercises are intended to allow the defender to bypass the feeling of threat and focus on the feeling of interaction, i.e., motion in unison, and thus to be able to make time in the midst of the sparring interchange.

Lastly, the concepts of progressively undefined one-step and the attack combination building described above can be combined. The initial exercise is called "dodge-punch" and consists of each partner taking turns in the attacking and defensive role. The rule is to limit the attack to stepping punch only, that is, the attacker's stance must change legs completely. The defender is limited to shifting without blocking, with the intent to arrive at a location from which their subsequent stepping punch will have the greatest chance to succeed. This exercise is both enjoyable, and when driven by a rapid count, quite aerobic.

The next stage of this is to allow parrying along with shifting on the defender's part and two attacks of any sort on the attacker's part, essentially the first stage of combination building. This is progressively built up into the full 5-step attack combination of fake, lead-in, main technique, follow-on, and cover-out techniques. Once this is achieved, and the defender can "field" the attacks successfully, the defender then begins to attempt to "cut" into these attacks with counterattacks. In the end, this is what is termed "directed free" sparring—attacking and defending roles are predetermined, but all else is undefined, provided the attack is performed in a single intention (usually a single breath).

It should be noted that this type of training—undefined, multiple-step directed attack/defense—is one of the most difficult exercises in sparring possible. In true free sparring, the defender always has the option to launch a pre-emptive attack, and this possibility tends to inhibit the attacker's freedom. In the directed free sparring case, the attacker has no such concern. For successful training, senior students (e.g. higher-ranked kyu grades) should assume the defender's role while junior students (lower-ranked kyu grades) assume the attacker's. When the first kyu brown belt can handle easily the 6th kyu student's directed free attacks, then it is time to increase the challenge by working with the next most experienced level of attacker.

The central problem in sparring for most students is the problem of the "Arms of Shiva" (portrayed as a statue with a multitude of arms, each with a weapon ready to strike). Thus the beginner sees not a single person ready to attack, but rather a huge universe of techniques, any and all of which can arrive at any time, and all of which need to have a counter prepared. To solve (avoid) this problem, one can analogize the attacker into a single attack force, somewhat like a locomotive bearing down at full speed.

By simplifying the situation from the attempt to react to the specific attack into one where all that is required is "to get off the railroad track," the mind is calmed and centralized. Follow this shifting movement with a swift and committed re-entry into attack range, and the specific counter attack will emerge spontaneously as the target reveals itself.

Chapter 10
Counterattack

In general, given that humans are bilaterally symmetrical, for any given one-limbed attack, the defensive body shift can be classified into one of four alternatives. Two of these relate to the opponent and two to oneself.

For example, given a right stepping-in or flowing punch starting from a left stance, the opponent ends with the right foot and hand forward, and the hip making a partial counterclockwise rotation. This sets up two regions of space split by the attack vector—the inside-front or chest area *(omote)* and the outside-back area *(ura)* (see figure 11). Therefore, one's answering movements to this attack must move into one of these two areas.

In each of these two regions, since the defender is also bilaterally symmetrical, there are two methods of movement to enter the area—a crossing or sliding entry *(irimi)* and a turning or circling entry *(tenkan)*. These terms are taken from *aikido* and define the same type of entry points into an opponent's space, albeit for the end purpose of (usually) throwing the opponent. Initially, however, the procedures in *aikido* and karate are similar. In our example of a right flowing stepping punch, stepping to the back of (behind) the opponent with the left foot forward is an outside circular shift, and with the right foot, it is an outside sliding shift.

If we entered to the front (moving to our own right), the right foot forward lead is an inside circular shift, and the left foot lead, an inside shift that crosses the opponent's stance (see figure 12). The movements used can be shifts, steps, spins, or any combination in order to adjust to the opponent's movements.

The most important part to understand, however, is the relationship between the two body centers. Primacy needs to be given to placement of the body, since that will determine the selection of countering technique as well as the safety of employment. Stated another way: Rule #1: don't get hit.

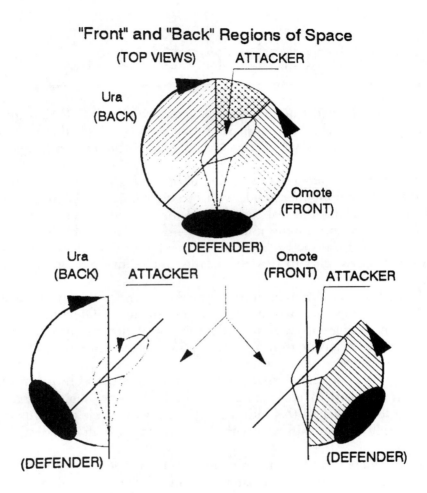

**Figure 11
Omote & Ura**

Top view of so-called "front" and "back" regions of the opponent's space as labeled by the defender during a lead hand punch attack; overlap region at the attacker's back quarter can be either (although usually Back/Ura), depending on the defender's motion.

Advanced Karate-Do 77

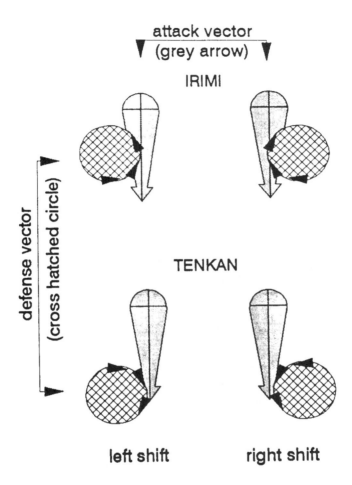

**Figure 12
Counterattack Vectors**

Top views of the circular power flows in response to a focused linear (thrust) attack: Turning (tenkan) rides the attack and stretches it while slipping to the side. Crossing (irimi) goes around/under the attack and foreshortens it by direct counterattack.

Perhaps the easiest visualization is that *tenkan* moves attempt to place the attacker's energy on the outside of a turning wheel of which the defender is the hub, wrapping the attack around it to both overextend as well as pull it off-line. The *irimi* movement attempts to reverse the attacker's momentum, generally by deflecting upward so that the attacker's feet slide out from under them while crossing the opponent's centerline.

10.1 Outside Shifting

To understand this method of defensive movement with the shift to the outside (toward the opponent's back), as an example visualize the spatial relationship between the two sets of hips as if they were two spinning tops.

The opponent's spin is already determined by the right-handed attack, in this case, counterclockwise. The *turning* countermove will spin the defender's hip so that if they touched, the place they touch would be moving jointly and together. In our example (we being the defender), the outside circular countermove will step to the rear (our left) and spin the hip (since our left leg is moving forward) clockwise. If the two sets of hips touched, the rotation of both hips would mesh like a set of gears except for the possible speed mismatch. On the other hand, the outside slide response moves our right foot to the rear (crossing right feet) and rotates the hip counterclockwise so that if the hips touched, their rotations would clash. Practice the following specific techniques (attacker in left front stance, defender in natural stance):

Attack: Right (flowing) stepping-in punch

1st Defense (turning to the back, *tenkan ura*): Left foot steps to the left front (right foot adjusts), left arm outside forearm block, follow with immediate left hand flowing punch counter to the head.

2nd Defense (crossing to the back, *irimi ura*): Right foot steps to the left front, right arm inside ridge hand block, follow with left spinning short back kick to the ribs under the punch.

3rd Defense (also crossing to the back, *irimi ura*): Left foot slides in to your left front, right hand sliding outside parry and grab with simultaneous right knee roundhouse kick into the ribs under the punch.

10.2 Inside Shifting

Shifting to the front or inside is more difficult to explain, since the analogy of the top will not work. In shifting to the open front of the attacker, movements that pull out or extend the attacking limb and its associated hip are generally turning movements while those that bypass it to project force directly into the opponent's center are crossing movements (see fig. 13).

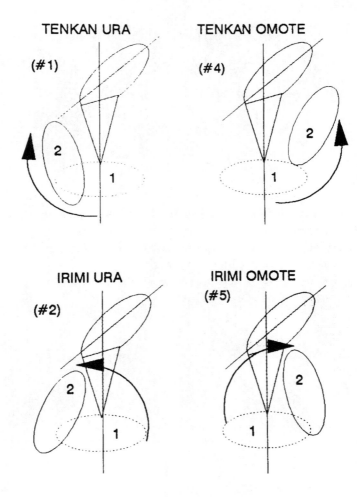

**Figure 13
Examples**

Top view of counterattack examples against a focused lunge punch using the two regions and two trajectories described in the previous figures and techniques from the text. Attacker in gray, defender's initial position in dotted outline (1), position after the initial defensive shift in solid outline (2).

4th Defense (turning in front, *tenkan omote*): Right foot steps to the right front. Turn counterclockwise with left hand knife hand block, ending in left foot forward back stance facing almost the same direction as the opponent; follow with right hand reverse punch to the face.

5th Defense (crossing in front, *irimi omote*): Left foot steps to the right front; evade by ducking the punch, spin clockwise with a right back elbow to the opponent's ribs under the punch.

Note again that the operative actions that define a movement as either crossing or turning are the relative force directions, not which foot actually moves or what technique is used. Also, the areas labeled front and back are defined by the opponent's hips, or alternatively by the target area position, not by which limb is attacking, e.g., if the attack were a left hand reverse punch with the right foot lead, the opponent's *front* and *back* are defined as above.

More explicitly, a right foot forward step implies a counterclockwise hip, unless the attacker actually spins the hip in the opposite direction (as in the extended counterpunch to a reversed hip position). The actual techniques used to counter might change in that one might rather go with an outside circular shift to stay "outside" the arm and still have open body target for the counter (e.g., knife hand block followed by a kidney punch), or even an inside sliding shift (e.g., cross parry with short counterpunch into the armpit).

With all these variations, and there are many more, what the hips are doing will not change, but the exact shape of the counter will. With an explicit demonstration of the principles, and emphasis on the movement itself rather than the actual hand techniques, the students should begin to grasp the basic concepts of both the rotational and the more linear sliding defensive shifts.

10.3 Snap Shifts

Several things should become clear with practice of the above techniques.

First, outside shifting is safer than inside shifting and allows more time for the counterattack. Second, crossing movements put more power into the opponent (greater impact since the hip directions mutually collide) than turning movements. Third, following the initial entry mode, a turning movement can change into a crossing movement, and vice versa, by rotating the hips back the other way to spring the counter technique. This switch will force a one-two timing mode that can succeed only if the opponent is sufficiently unbalanced so that the attacker cannot continue smoothly.

To practice the shifting in a more free form manner, the pendulum training mentioned earlier can be adapted to become a positioning training. In this exercise, the partners take turns attacking each other with any single count stepping or sliding in attack, using any technique aimed at any target. The defender makes an appropriate defensive shift and parry. Then the roles reverse without either person adjusting stance, direction, or position (see the dodge-punch exercise discussion in the chapter on timing). After about a dozen movements, this becomes a practice in learning not only how to shift so as to maximally frustrate an attack, but also in how to maximize the subsequent counterattack potential with appropriate techniques.

A danger that may occur with this type of circular shifting is that the mutuality of movement and timing results in the inability to pre-empt a follow-on attack, producing repeated "mutual attacks," i.e., the defender's counter occurs simultaneously with the attacker's second attack in free sparring instead of the desired win by the defender. There are several ways to deal with this problem, and which method is used depends on the linkage selected between the parry or block and the counterattack—simultaneous, sequential, or overlapping.

With simultaneous timing in the parry and counter, there is no problem since both partners focus their techniques together.

With an overlapping linkage, the block must be completed at or before the attacker's initial focus, and the counterattack must focus on the attacker's relaxation from the initial movement.

For the sequential linkage, the counterattack must focus before the attacker can produce a second focus. To do this, the defensive shift itself must be "snapped." This means that the leg and hip tensions that actually drive the shift are set up early and held until the attacker is committed to the attack vector. Then the leg holding a braking tension in the shift direction is slightly lifted, and the shift occurs instantly, feeling as if it were snapped into place. The block is simultaneously executed with the same speed, and the counterattack fired immediately.

With overlapping techniques, the block is somewhat softer, and the timing is such that the shift itself provides the starting power for the counterattack.

For circular or stepping shifts, the fastest snap shifts can be accomplished with inside tensions similar to *sanchin dachi* or *hangetsu dachi*.

For slide shifts, using outside tensions similar to *kiba dachi* work well.

In all cases, setting up the tension ahead of time will permit the defender to wait longer for the attacker to be more fully committed and thus less able to redirect the attack once it is launched. This last concept is critical for generating effective counterattacks or combinations.

10.4 Two-Step Shifting

Another type of shifting is two-step shifting, still with the proviso that the entire shift occur in one breath. Two-step shifting can be done with either one and one-half timing ("and-one") or with sequential ("one-two") timing.

The operational concept comes most directly from *aikido*, in which it is said, "Enter triangularly, deflect circularly, and finish squarely." So the two-step shift can be considered a triangular entry into the opponent in response to the opponent's advance.

The best analogy for the actual feel of this shift is that of running up to a wall at a slant, partially going up it with one step and then using the wall to change directions back towards the center of the room. On the floor, this translates into a "skateboard" style of hip movement in which a foot is planted (somewhat like a ski pole) and the hips banked off of it back into the opponent. This works best with the overlapping timing referred to above. Using sequential timing allows the opponent a chance to redirect the follow up attack back onto line and will require more energetic blocking as a result.

The trajectory traced on the floor, however, should be a right triangle whose right angle is on that point formed by the placement of the banking foot. To retreat in the initial movement is to defeat the entire process.

10.5 Retreat

The techniques used as examples have entries on the forward 45 degree movement lines. Lateral shifts and shifts along the back 45 degree lines also are possible and will fall into the above classification scheme depending on the hip rotations and movement direction, but the timing and feeling will be slightly different (as will the exact techniques).

These methods complete the two basic types of shifts—direct and turning—off of the attack line.

A third method of shifting—a linear escape to one's rear directly away from the attacker—can break off or at least delay the engagement and is, therefore, not a sufficient response to an attack in and of itself.

Additionally, movement towards the rear produces both a difficult psychological and physical problem: How does one reverse the mental and physical momentum so as to counterattack the opponent in time?

Stated another way: How can one prevent the opponent from retaining the initiative and so suppress a counterattack? This question can only be answered satisfactorily if the defender does not disconnect from the opponent's attack, but remains physically and mentally coordinated with it. This linkage between the partners then produces one application of direct backwards movement that can be performed successfully: To "stretch" the opponent into an over-extension before entry on one of the angles. This sort of shifting can only be accomplished with very good timing and while facing a short attack, i.e., not a fully developed charge built with well-linked combinations.

Direct forward counterattacks will not succeed unless one outweighs one's opponent and doesn't mind the crunch of bone on bone (as occasionally happens with beginners in free sparring training), or has superior timing (pre-emptive strikes) and generally longer limbs.

It must be remembered that the most efficient block is the one that doesn't need to be made. The parry is somewhat less efficient, and the least efficient is the power block.

This, in fact, is a central tenet in Bruce Lee's art of *Jeet Kune Do*—simultaneous parry and counter technique by the most simple timing and method possible.

In basic training, however, the blocks generally are taught in reverse order so that the student can stabilize the hips, but progression in learning also involves progression in skill.

There is one method of useful retreat that can be practiced—that of "riding the cowcatcher." Consider the attacker as simplified into a oncoming locomotive running down a railroad track. If one tries to run backwards along the track, the case is hopeless; one cannot outrun the attacker. If, on the other hand, one jumps onto the cowcatcher, the train may go as fast as it wishes and one is never run over. How to do this? Simply have the students pay attention to the foot movement pattern of their partner and exactly mirror it, both in time and in space. For the hand techniques, simply reply as if in a mirror, the defender's right hand to the attacker's left hand and vice versa, not attempting to do anything but simply frustrate the attacks. In order to prevent this from having no resolution (a danger since this can be quite seductive), one must realize that there is no way to get off the train gently—one must jump off.

In other words, any side step movement that simultaneously continues to retreat will never provide the opening desired since the attacker can easily follow. Two-step shifting is the only way to reliably and effectively get off the track and counterattack.

10.6 Attack

The tactics reviewed above refer to counterattack, since they all require an initial motion from the opponent to intercept. An immobile opponent is the most dangerous, since there is no indication of either the timing or the technique. Nevertheless, there are occasions when one cannot wait and must attack, most commonly with multiple opponents.

Attack is, by definition, pre-emptive and either finds or creates an opening through the opponent's guard to strike a vulnerable target.

Most simply, one can just move in around the opponent's lead hand, and strike. However, it is very rare that such single shot attacks can succeed against an experienced fighter.

The next level is a combination of attacks that are directed so as to build momentum and finally break through into the target zone by overwhelming the defense. Tactically, one can visualize the opponent as a marionette, with the strings moving the limbs being controlled by one's own movements. As the attacker moves, this implies movement by the opponent, and such movement can be taken advantage of. If the defender has good timing and moves freely, this too will fail. Then one must interdict the freedom to move by actively trapping the defending limb (jamming or grabbing) while launching the attack that that limb would normally have handled.

Failing this, one must attack the limbs themselves—as Musashi puts it, "injuring the corners"—on the way to the finishing attack.

If all this fails, one is left only with attempting to get the opponent to attack an offered target, and countering the movement with the entries mentioned in the previous section.

Bruce Lee's *Jeet Kune Do* labels these methods as 1) Simple Angular Attack–SAA, 2) Attack By Combination–ABC, 3) Limb Immobilization Attack (hand or foot)–LIA, 4) Progressive Indirect Attack–PIA, and 5) Attack By Drawing–ABD. These five methods are again on a continuum that sets the initial contact point with the opponent farther and farther away from the target center as one moves through the series, and what one uses will depend on the opponent's reactions.

True skill is reflected in the ability to switch tactics smoothly and naturally during an interchange of techniques.

Chapter 11
Sparring Tactics

Sparring is a method of practicing fighting techniques and tactics in a relatively controlled learning environment. It is usually conceived as an attempt to balance the competing desires for realism and safety. In JKA-style sparring, the compromises have included restricting the legal techniques to primarily medium to long range ballistic punching and kicking techniques, outlawing grappling methods, and refusing to recognize small scale technique, irrespective of their effectiveness in a real confrontation. Further, there was an explicit desire to develop a competitive method equivalent to the contest methods of kendo and judo. Thus there arose the problem of how to teach appropriate tactics suitable for winning contests with the restricted technique set. Since this was essentially a new martial art, some model was needed.

It is well known that many of the developers of JKA-style Shotokan karate had kendo backgrounds. It seems logical to ask whether kendo might illuminate the tactics taught to students over the past decades of JKA-style *kumite* competition. I believe that this is in fact the case, and that in specific, the *kata* of kendo provided almost move-for-move models for karate sparring tactics. In the following sections, I will show the relevant portions of the kendo *kata*, and in parallel, the karate applications of the principle shown in that *kata*.

Kendo *kata* are performed by two individuals in a very formalized setting, with minutely prescribed steps for entering the performance area, bowing, placement of the weapons, recognition of the opponent, establishment of the correct distancing, etc. I will ignore the formalisms and present only the actual encounters that are the heart of each *kata*. These are more equivalent to one-step sparring demonstrations than *kata*, as usually understood by the karate practitioner. The short descriptions of the tactics are quoted from Budden P., <u>Looking at a Far Mountain. A Study of Kendo kata</u>, pp 35 – 36, which I used as a reference for this work (see Bibliography). In all cases the attacker is coming from the left and is called *Uchidachi*, and the defender (and winner of each one-step encounter) is on the right, and called *Shidachi*. Budden states "Although not always obviously visible when watching the performance of the *kata*, and in particular that at the highest level, there exists a series of signals or triggers that are of paramount importance in learning the cause and effect of the *kata*. Although it is stated that the controlling influence of the *kata* is made by *Uchidachi*, *Shidachi* has to get a reaction from *Uchidachi* in order to perform the correct movements."

Further, Budden says: "It cannot be stressed enough that these signals should in no way alter the timing of tempo of the *kata*, as they are subtle movements that become less and less apparent as the practitioner becomes more and more fluent. In the final event they become part of the very feeling of the *kata*, invisible but integral. However, when first learning *kata* movements, they should not be made unless they are made apparent, as this establishes at a very early level this true cause and effect. Thus if no reaction is given to a situation, no action should be taken."

This relates directly to the karate concept of pressure (*tsumeai*), in which one person applies psychological pressure on his partner via adjusting the interval, defined in both time and distance (*ma-ai*) to evoke a suitable attack for which the counter has been pre-prepared.

This is perhaps a good place to consider the term "*ma-ai*" in more detail. The modern understanding is that *ma-ai* distinctly means only "distance" or "distancing" and is separate from timing *per se*. In modern Japanese, "*ma*" means interval all by itself and can be used in the context of describing pauses [intervals] in *kata*. However, there is also the second character "*ai*", which means mutual or together. Thus the word can be translated mutual timing and further implies that it is expressed through distance. I think that the raw translation into (a timeless) "distance" is a mistranslation of the Japanese concept of *ma-ai*. Both my kyudo and my aikido teachers have noted that while *ma-ai* is commonly used to refer to distance, in these martial arts at least, it means exactly what it says: mutual interval, mutual rhythm, or in other words, harmonization. The most appropriate *ma-ai* for two people who start and move slowly will be closer together than for two people who are swift. It will also be farther apart for those who see slowly vs. those who have fast reaction times. In kumite, it is not as if one player is attacking a static object, like a wall, from which a certain distance should be kept. The player is engaging a moving, breathing, conniving "other". And it is toward the "other" that a person is adjusting, plotting, engaging, or reacting to. Timing must most certainly come into play. It is important for the reader to get out of the closed box of thinking that distance is all that matters, when it is the time-space-mind "interval" that is important, and is to be wrapped up in the word "*ma-ai*."

Before getting into the actual *kata*, I must acknowledge Mr. David Russell (*uchidachi*, in the dark *keiko-gi*) and Mr. Eddie Barnes, Jr. (*shida-*

chi, in the light *keiko-gi*) of the Triangle Kendo and Iaido club for posing for the kendo *kata*, and Mr. Steve Baxley, of the Shotokan Dojo in Dothan, Alabama, for consenting to be my partner in the karate examples.

11.1 Evade Backward: Tachi-no-kata Ipponme (*men-nuki-men*); to draw an attack so that it falls just short and follow-up by entering over it, maintaining a continuing threat.

> [Budden] From the right *jodan* position at the center meeting point, *Shidachi* makes a slight downward movement as if about to cut, hence causing *Uchidachi* to commit himself to the full blooded *men* cut. *Shidachi* then applies *nuki* to avoid this attack.

From the karate perspective, this kata is translated into the often seen linear dodging or swaying directly to the rear calculated to make the attack just fall short, then following up with a counter into the void left by the opponent's miss, striking before a follow-up attack can be made. While the kendo kata does not involve a parry, in karate, since there are two hands available, and since the intent is to press in over the opponent's attack, one hand can be used to press down the attack during the counter. Here I show a lunge punch answered by an evasion, then a cover with a sliding counterpunch. Note that the cover is not a parry of the attack, but an immobilization of the attacker. Recall also that the attack must be invited or triggered to occur, both in this example and in the following ones for the other kata.

11.2 Evade Sideward: Tachi-no-kata Nihonme (kote-nuki-kote); to slip an attack sideways and counter quickly.

[Budden] In the centre chudan position, Shidachi slightly raises his point or presses the Uchidachi sword to the left, almost as an invitation to Uchidachi to cut his kote, which he does.

From the karate perspective, this *kata* can be translated into a counter that slips behind the attacker's arm, this time by dodging sideways instead of to the back. With the shorter *ma-ai* in karate, again a lateral covering parry can be used with one hand while the other simultaneously executes the counter. Here I show a sliding counterpunch attack answered with a sideslip and a counterpunch, again using a covering movement with the other hand.

11.3 Thrust Forward: Tachi-no-kata Sanbonme (tsuki-osaeuke-tsuki): to force an attack, cover, and drive directly in through opposition:

> [Budden] At the *chudan* position, raised from *gedan*, *Shidachi* comes up to *chudan* slightly later than *Uchidachi*, inviting *Uchidachi* to *tsuki*, or thrust.

The kendo kata actually consists of five steps forward by the defender that constitutes a charge (only the first and last are shown above). This kata is representative of the more-or-less famous "shotokan charge" that takes an attack as an opportunity to suppress the opponent and drive in with repeated thrusts and covers, overwhelming any attempt to either retreat or to parry. In this case, both partners use real parries. Here I show an attempted front kick, parried to the side and answered with repeated counterpunches and cross step entries with pressing blocks, eventually overwhelming the initial attacker's ability to parry and/or evade.

11.4 FlowAround: Tachi-no-kata Yohonme (aiuchi-tsuki-nagashiuke-men); to stay attached to an attack and flow around its continuation by turning the corner.

[Budden] After the Aiuchi, which should have the feeling of Uchidachi going into jodan and cutting (Uchidachi doesn't know the length so attacks) and that of Shidachi realizing and revealing now the length of his sword, reacting by cutting with a feeling of stop, into aiuchi (simultaneously cut) and then down into chudan. Shidachi relaxes his kamae thus slightly inviting the thrust of Uchidachi.

Here the concept of not detaching from the opponent, but instead continuing to control the attacking arm no matter how it tries to avoid being parried is stressed. In the karate case, since there are two arms at least in action, both the initial clash and the follow-up are more complex than the kendo case, but the attitude and body feel remains the same. The attack is a lunge punch followed immediately upon receiving the block with a back fist by the same limb. The answer involves a soft outside block that does not disconnect from the attacker's forearm, but by staying in contact can flow up into an up block and circular deflection during the counterpunch response.

11.5 Parry Large: Tachi-no-kata Gohonme (men-suriage-men); to deflect and counter an attack in one intention.

[Budden] From the raised chudan (seigan), Shidachi pushes slightly forward seme with his ken sen towards the kobushi of Uchidachi, the left fist area of the left jodan kamae or opens his ken sen slightly right side. Uchidachi reacts by cutting men.

The principle here is to use the preparation motion of the counterattack to itself provide the parry. The timing is such that the counter happens during the interval between the opponent's first attack and his attempt at a continuation. This is perhaps the most common tactic to answer any face attack. Here I show a lead hand jab that the attacker intends to follow with a counterpunch (the commonly expected one-two attack). The defender intercepts the jab with one hand and throws a counterpunch into the interval within the attacker's combination with the other.

11.6 Parry Small: Tachi-no-kata Ropponme (kote-suriage-kote); to force and then counter a small-scale attack as an entry to dominant control.

[Budden] Shidachi applies pressure twice, firstly from gedan in chudan causing Uchidachi to back at speed into jodan and back further into chudan, and again by this feeling of pressure forcing Uchidachi to commit himself to a rather hasty kote attack.

In this illustration, it is shown that an upset opponent may only give a small-scale attack, but that even this provides sufficient movement to be quickly disposed of. Here I show the attacker giving a small lead hand jab, which is answered by a sliding parry-grab and a stepping entry into a punch.

11.7 Mutual Attack: Tachi-no-kata Nanahonme (tsuki-osae-men-aiuchi-do); to suppress small-scale attack inducing over-commitment followed by passing through the opponent's attack.

[Budden] Shidachi again inviting a thrust by slightly raising his point and on the thrust, on upwards into a parry. Aituski (simultaneous thrust).

The total commitment to the attack, passing through the oncoming counter, is often stressed to the karate student. It is believed that in this manner, the person with the clearest mind will win, since there is no thought of defense to slow down the entry into the opponent's space. Attempts to do this by two similarly skilled individuals in tournament can result in long sequences of simultaneous sliding counterpunches with both sides landing the attack, but neither side able to claim the point. For this concept, the example is a stepping punch attack answered with a stepping short counterpunch, both sides advancing into the encounter, but the defender bypassing the attack vector slightly to one side.

11.8 Slip Right: Kodachi-no-kata Ipponme (men-nagashiuke-men); to enter closely beside the attack.

[Budden] Shidachi makes Uchidachi react by the pressure of seme at the kobushi of Uchidachi, with the feeling of Irimi (entering).

The short sword forms are the closest that shotokan style sparring permits in small-scale technique. These kata form analogies to either one-handed counters or counters that include pressing or gripping control of the attacker's limb(s). In this case, one can envision a single-armed parry followed by a back fist counterattack answering a lead hand attack to the face.

11.9 Slip Left: Kodachi-no-kata Nihonme (osae-men-gyaku-nagashiuke-men-hijitori); to force a large scale attack, counter, and control closely.

> [Budden] Shidachi, by trying to hold down the spirit (will) of Uchidachi and Uchidachi backward into waki gamae, Shidachi forward again by seme and irimi Uchidachi reacting men cut.

This time, instead of moving to the inside of the attack, the defender moves to the outside, and maintains control after the counterstrike, similar to the applications of the Tekki kata or in how one applies a foot sweep. In this case, the defender explicitly presses into the attacker to force a response. Here the defender as initiator slides in, causing the attacker (who is responding in this case) to step back and then front kick with the moving leg. The attacking leg is parried, the support leg is swept, and the arm is captured during the counter.

11.10 Suppress: Kodachi-no-kata Sanbonme (men-sotouke-gyakudo-osaeuke-kansetsuwaza); to continuously slap aside attacks while establishing central control.

|| [Budden] Shidachi by gedan, invites via this open unguarded position to cut his men, a welcoming invitation to attack. ||

Since this kata ends in an elbow lock, it cannot be used as is. What one sees is an almost contemptuous smacking aside of the attacker's strikes culminating in complete control and immobilization. Again, I use a one-two attack for the karate example in which the defender uses the lead hand to parry first one and then the other while entering into a throw.

Sport kendo also has contributed to the technical lexicon of JKA-style sparring, and a review of a good basic kendo book e.g., Sasamori & Warner, *This is Kendo* (see bibliography) will show a classification of techniques that can be used to construct attack and counterattack combinations for any arbitrary situation. The concepts of *Harai Waza* (Warding Off Techniques), *Nidan* or *Sandan Waza* (2- or 3-step Techniques) and *Nuki Waza* (Feinting and Dodging Techniques) will be very familiar to experienced tournament players. Nevertheless, these methods refer to kendo *shinai*-sparring, and do not deal directly with the same concepts as the kendo *kata*. *This is Kendo* demonstrates a sports sparring approach in which it is assumed that the situation is not touch-and-bleed as with a real sword, but simply intense sparring. The classifications given are of *waza* (techniques) rather than tactics or strategy. Real Japanese swords aren't used in the western fashion of chopping at each other in the manner beloved of Hollywood, nor are the techniques illustrated in Sasamori applicable as demonstrated to real swords. In the same way, one must be aware that karate sparring methods do not translate directly into street fighting or self-defense skill.

In summary, these kendo *kata* express principles of tactics and/or attitude that apply in a relatively clear and obvious way to those seen in classical shotokan sparring encounters. Study of them under a kendo teacher will reward the student with not only a stronger sense of *ma-ai* but also with a sharpening of the psychological awareness needed in sparring. Facing a three-foot length of curved oak is a good method to ensure one's attention.

Chapter 12
Styles and Methods

How one trains and is trained differs with the national character of the country of origin of the martial art (including its philosophical and ethical basis), the ability of the student, and the character of the instructor.

The national character aspect perhaps can be illustrated with examples from China and Japan—not because these are the only ones, or even the best, but because the dichotomy I propose here can be seen relatively clearly in American schools claiming these origins.

Basically, in the most extreme cases, Chinese arts show a somewhat informal, looser, and more extensive style of training, while Japanese arts are more intensive, with a greater emphasis on repeated practice of the individual basic techniques in an atmosphere of greater formality. As with any generality, especially one this broad, there will be many exceptions; however, setting this aside, one can make the argument without referring to nationalities at all, but only to methodologies. For convenience sake, I will use the terms "Japanese" and "Chinese" simply as illustrative, rather than definitive, terms for the methods described.

So, to continue the analogies, in a Japanese school, one may practice a reverse punch many thousands of times in order to get it just right, trying for the "perfect punch," whereas in a Chinese-style school, one may practice a thousand different variants of the reverse punch in order to apply it to any situation, i.e., a "sufficiently effective" punch. Okinawan styles and *dojo* are, logically enough, often somewhere between these two extremes, reflecting their geography and historical associations.

12.1 Dojo Sparring

The styles of free sparring also exhibit a dichotomy. The hard Japanese styles tend to be "one-shot" artists, striving for a single and clearly overpowering "kill." Many Chinese styles, on the other hand, try to hit an opponent so often from so many different directions in so short a time that the defenses are simply overwhelmed and the opponent is defeated by the accumulated damage. This even can be seen in the popular martial arts movies of the two cultures, Japanese *chambara* (samurai) films and somewhat misnamed Chinese *kung-fu* films. In both film types, generally there is a climactic duel at the end. The Japanese film duel consists of long periods of immobility between the two protagonists, followed by a single swift and sharp conflict that is immediately over with the death of one. The Chinese film duel consists of a running fight over many minutes, with both parties to the duel receiving and giving many "hits." The end finally comes when the evil antagonist allows a hole to develop in an otherwise flawless technical screen (usually through pride), and the hero adds the final straw. Both parties usually are near death.

In empty-hand sparring, the Japanese-style schools tend to be cleaner and clearer in their techniques while the Chinese tend to display more continuous movement. Tournament scoring styles also reflect this. Japanese compete in one-point matches while the Chinese compete for the maximum number of points within a certain time limit. Regrettably, this can lead to misunderstandings, hurt feelings, and even injury if unprepared and uncontrolled sparring is allowed between individuals coming from these different styles. Each views the other as breaking unwritten rules. The Japanese stylist sees the Chinese stylist as not respecting or acknowledging a valid attack by stopping the action after a successful score. The response is then to hit harder until the Chinese stylist is forced to stop by pain or injury. On the other hand, the Chinese stylist sees the Japanese stylist as either not interacting (i.e., a type of cowardice by not wanting to spar—running away) or intending actually to damage. The response is either to quit or to push closer and press harder to get inside the opponent's technique with more of a self-defense attitude to force the action. The result is jammed fingers and toes with occasional broken noses or ribs, and neither party accomplishes any learning. The only result is that each is confirmed in the belief that the other cheats.

An exercise the Japanese stylist can undertake to better understand the Chinese point of view is "30-second attack." In this, one partner holds a large pad, and the other must attack continuously and with varied techniques for 30 seconds at full speed. While it is easy to perform a flurry of attacks lasting some five to 10 seconds, 30 seconds force a different type of free sparring that is much closer to the Chinese methods. This can be expanded with multiple partners holding pads who attempt to "smother" the trainee with them unless held off with continuous techniques.

12.2 Kata

The dichotomy between constant movement and staccato impact also is reflected in the traditional forms (*kata*) of the schools. The Chinese, with some exceptions (most notably in the "external" hard styles), tend to have a few forms (sometimes only one, like Yang family *tai chi chuan*) that are long, extensive, continuous, circular, and take a long time both to learn and to perform. Additionally, such forms may appear somewhat esoteric in their movements, since they have an overlay of physical culture and hygiene as part of their rationale.

Some of the beginning hard style Chinese forms have essentially calisthenic movements rather than combat movements in them, e.g., full splits on the floor.

The Japanese styles, on the other hand, have many forms, each of which can be performed in one or two minutes. These *kata* of Okinawan origin tend to be directly related to combat and emphasize focus and impact. Even with this larger number of *kata*, the Japanese stylist generally will concentrate on perfecting only one form at a time over a period of years. The techniques are less calisthenic since they come from Okinawan fighter roots. The techniques also are more stylized because the overlay in this case is the Japanese formalism, styling, and aesthetic sense rather than either gymnastics or simple practicality.

In JKA shotokan *kata* especially, with the previously noted background of kendo and the emphasis on non-contact tournament sparring, the close range techniques of the Okinawan forbears such as Shorin-ryu have been expanded to sword range, leading to difficulties in interpretation. The distancing implied in Okinawan *kata* is much more aligned with knife-fighting ranges, and it as at such ranges that the applications and techniques derived from these *kata* make the most sense.

12.3 Emphasis

One of the major things an instructor must settle clearly is the balance of training between *kata* (formal exercises), *kihon* (basics), and *kumite* (sparring). The proportions selected and relative emphases are based on the goals the instructor seeks to attain with the students. So a question that needs to be answered is, "Is this to be predominantly a self-defense class, a self-development class, or a tournament class?" The answer to this question is likely to be some personal mixture unique to the instructor. With this answer, the appropriate tools can be selected.

For self-defense emphasis, *kata* is an appropriate training method, emphasizing the dissection and practice of the various tactics, combinations, and sequences with partners. For the instructor who is more interested in teaching the *do* of *Karate-do*, *kihon* is the best initial tool, since repeated practice of simplified basic movements encourages the student towards self-reflection, concentrated improvement, and perfection of each technique in an idealized and almost meditative environment. This can be followed by repeated *kata* practice viewed as a movement exercise. In other words, this type of training can been seen as a form of kickboxing combined with yoga, emphasizing breathing, posture, attention, and repetition, all oriented toward producing changes in mental state.

For the tournament oriented instructor, extended free sparring and the practice of *kumite* techniques appropriate to the particular set of sport rules used are started as soon as the student learns the rudiments of punching, kicking, blocking, and shifting.

Tournament sparring is a relatively recent invention. Historically, fights occurred between followers of various martial arts schools, but these had much more serious consequences than the losing of a trophy. In Okinawa, the training was predominantly *kata*, thus supporting the goal of self-defense. With the export of karate to Japan, the art was transformed from *karate-jutsu* (China-hand technique) to *karate-do* (empty-hand way), and gained a Zen Buddhist aspect. This change attempted to enlarge *karate-do* into a method of attaining enlightenment and transcending the fear of death, similar to other Japanese *budo* arts.

Additionally, the art was changed physically to become a method more suitable for group training of children in schools. Accordingly, the main training method changed from *kata* and self-defense applications to the perfection of *kihon* as a method of improving the physical and moral character of the students.

The creation of free sparring arose from karate's interaction with judo and kendo (see the previous chapter). As with these Japanese arts, the emphasis originally was on *ippatsu*, or winning with one overwhelming technique. Thus, the Japanese style of tournament training in karate is based on *kihon*, with points awarded for the best and clearest application of basic technique in a fluid situation.

In America, the sport element has tended to overtake the other elements. Modern *Tae Kwon Do* especially—currently practiced as a sport form—encourages techniques in a framework of restrictive rules that make an exciting spectator sport match—an idea in stark contrast to karate's more general self-defense training and training in the perfection of the basic techniques. The preferred tournament style has become one of scoring multiple points within a set time frame, which obviates combat reality.

All three ways of training are valid by their own assumptions, but even though there are superficial similarities between these, all three are fundamentally different in outlook and execution. The instructor must be clear on what is desired so as to not mislead the students into believing they are learning self-defense when they actually are learning to win tournaments.

12.4 Rank

Measuring a student's progress and giving accurate feedback are necessary parts of any teaching process. Students naturally will compare themselves on a relative scale, and also seek to verify their understanding of the teacher's standards. To this end, ranking is used.

Some styles have only a minimal emphasis on rank. For example, in some Chinese soft styles like *tai chi chuan*, students may rank themselves simply by the number of years they've been training. In other schools, like some aikido federations, while there are *kyu* levels below the black belt, students wear only a white belt until *shodan*. This is a reflection of the older *menkyo-kaiden* (license) system of grading. In this system, one was either a beginner, a student, an instructor, or a master. In time, this was followed by the more familiar *kyu-dan* system, with multiple levels for students and for instructors. Part of the former system remains and can be seen in the terms for various instructor levels: *shidoin, renshi, kyoshi, hanshi*. These terms all imply the meaning of instructor but have various amounts of respect built into them, and now tend to go in step with the higher *dan* grades.

At the extreme, there are schools that have 10 levels below black belt, each with its own color of belt, occasionally with stripes across the ends to mark sub-levels, and 10 levels above black belt, each marked either with multiple stripes on the belt or different patterns of black, red, and white panels. For at least the *kyu* ranks, the colored belts act as a teaching convenience in that they divide the class into approximate ability levels. Then the instructor can teach a large mixed class of many ranks, asking, for example, the yellow belts to do one thing, the green belts to do that plus another added-on technique, the brown belts to add on even more, and the black belts to do the whole combination in reverse.

Such a separation permits everyone to train together, with everyone experiencing an appropriate level of difficulty and sharing an approximately equal level of frustration, thus building a *dojo* camaraderie that crosses all ranks.

Ranking itself presents a difficult ethical problem for the American commercial dojo: How can an instructor keep both high standards as well as sufficient students to pay the rent? In some cases, as noted above, this need has resulted in a proliferation of belt colors and a multiplicity of ranks, each of a sufficiently small step in skill that there is an adequate psychological reinforcement for the minimally motivated student, and simultaneously generating further bits of revenue from the test fee, the belt sale, the certificate fee, and the registration fee for the rank.

Schools that function within a university structure (e.g., a P.E. class or a student club) are spared the financial pressures, but have only a four year window for most of their students. Thus they have a constant recruiting problem and can remain locked into technically low levels of training.

Nevertheless, external ranking is needed to help the students understand their own progress. It is common that students' ability to see their errors and technical failings increases faster than their ability to correct them. Then the instructor is faced with the problem of discouraged students who believe they are actually getting worse through training rather than better. Explicit rankings help to combat this.

An analogy that may help the intermediate student is that of "carving a cube into a sphere." Training is the process of chopping off corners. Initially, the corners are large and easy to see, as is progress. Later, each corner cut off reveals three new corners, albeit smaller ones. This process is endless, and while an advanced student may appear to others of lesser experience to be a perfect sphere, the individual is often painfully aware of the many corners that still need polishing. Both receiving and giving ranking exams stabilize the perceptions and produce a reality check for both students and instructors.

In general terms, the following are some definitions for a Japanese-style karate rank advancement, both for *kyu* grades and for *dan* grades.

Throughout the *kyu* ranks, the student learns basics.

For the 8th and 7th *kyu* (and below for those that use more *kyu* levels) the requirement is knowledge of what the student is supposed to do with the techniques and a demonstrably clear understanding of the difference between the strike and thrust concepts, the lockout and snapback concepts, and the difference between front, back, and side stances during execution of the various techniques. This does not mean that techniques embodying each concept must be performed in perfect form. The student simply must demonstrate an understanding of the basic differences between the various concepts. Their back stance doesn't look like their front stance; their knife hand block in fact uses an open hand edge; their front kick, and roundhouse kick have trajectories that differ by about 90 degrees, their side snap kick has a different trajectory than their side thrust kick; etc.

Transition to green belt (6th *kyu*) requires precise, correct posture and technique trajectories and timing with no mistakes, even if without "full" power. The 5th and 4th *kyu* levels (also green belt) are more sophisticated refinements of this level as well as the beginning of free sparring and the growth of real speed and focus. Here, the instructor should expect correct shapes for every stance and fundamental technique. Further, sequential techniques should be cleanly sequential with no blurriness between when one technique ends and the next starts, e.g., up-block followed by counterpunch should have cleanly rotating hips, stable stance and a clear point at which the momentum changes from accept (block) to deliver (punch). This clarity is to be demonstrated in basic one-step sparring as well as in the *kata* appropriate for the grade.

Transition into brown belt (3rd *kyu*) is based on power—the clear expression of stance stability and force transmission from the floor to the target with all basic techniques. Strong legs without wobbling knees are a touchstone for their stances; commitment of the body weight moving both forward and backward without leaning are critical. Advancing nose first, or retreating tail-bone first are indicators that more training is needed before this level is passed.

The 2nd and 1st *kyu* levels round out the physical learning of the basics and stress application of the basics in varied situations, e.g., sparring. In practice this means clean entry from free-style stances into full basic stances for technique delivery followed by a balanced recovery for both individual and partner practice. At these ranks, the longer, historical and more advanced *kata* are practiced, carrying with them the requirement to be able to apply the principles of movement learned with basic techniques into complex techniques not obviously related to punching and kicking.

Within a university *dojo*, the schedule of training sessions is arranged to cover the material needed for each rank in a semester, resulting in about three ranking exams per year. The time progression should be about a year to a year and a half in each color for the *kyu* grades (white, green, and brown if using the 3 color *kyu* system), depending, of course, on individual ability. Between three and five years from beginner to first step black belt or *shodan* (assuming at least three, one-hour training periods a week for about 45 weeks per year) is a reasonable time frame. Alternatively, one can say that minimum of about 30 hours of training is required for each *kyu* ranking (somewhat more at and above brown belt). Rank progression faster than this is only possible for those students previously ranked in another martial art or for the rare exception of natural ability.

An analogy to the training process is calligraphy—the practice of writing perfect and beautiful letters. From the point of graduation from *kyu* to *dan* rank, what is developed is the writing of an original piece of literature. However, the practice of writing the individual letters themselves must not be neglected so that clarity, legibility, and beauty do not decay with time.

Transition into first *dan* includes a mental step that requires the conscious experience of *kensho*. This can occur when the person experiences with full awareness the release of a technique into an opening without having planned it consciously, i.e., right brain control rather than left brain. In performing individual techniques, it should appear that the techniques are "doing the person" rather than the person doing the techniques, i.e. completely internalized so that the individual almost is no longer capable of doing the techniques incorrectly, even with conscious effort to do them wrongly.

Transition to 2nd *dan* occurs when the person can at will enter this state (although maintaining it may be spotty) and spar effectively without preplanning the individual combinations. The student is almost "along for the ride," watching the body do its job while the mind considers strategy and non-verbally feels for a match between a collection of ingrained attack tactics and technique combinations and an opponent's dynamic posture. In this rank, the goal is to make the karate techniques "intuitive" rather than simply a learned skill.

The 3rd *dan* can be considered both the first teaching rank as well as the terminal technical rank and requires that the person have a clear knowledge of how to get a student to and through the 1st *kyu* to 1st *dan* transition, i.e., not only teach full mastery of all the basic techniques but also be able to induce the *kensho* experience. At this point, a truly personal style of karate begins to develop. The goal in this rank is to make one's technique "invisible" so that less trained opponents will not be able to predict or react in time to any movement.

The 4th *dan*, logically, is the ability to develop a 1st *dan* into a 2nd *dan*, i.e., make the chance occurrence of correct mental state (*munen*, no words; *mushin*, no mind) subject to will.

The 5th *dan* is the ability to create a 3rd *dan* instructor, i.e., the knowledge of how to teach someone how to teach.

It has been said that above 5th *dan* there is no longer technical or pedagogic progress, but only administrative advancement, i.e., the amount of work done for the association of which one is a member. However, with continuing practice, it can be expected that the instructor's overall skill will continue to improve, even if it radically changes in character due to age.

The reader may note differences between the set of requirements presented here for the various *dan* grades and those of other organizations. In my opinion, while the specific numbers given change, depending on the priorities of each of these organizations, the specific ranks are only relative shifts of what precise level of understanding and capability are needed for each grade.

For example, the World Karate-do Federation places teaching at 4th *dan* rather than 3rd and emphasizes a research requirement for the 5th through 8th *dan*, reserving 9th and 10th as service grades. In contrast, the Shotokan Karate of America stops at 5th *dan*, and has no higher grades. The overall range of expertise between senior practitioners in the two organizations is similar—only the assigned numbers and the step sizes they use for classification has changed.

One universal benchmark seems to be mastery of basics at the *kyu* to *dan* transition, which includes mastery of the mental basic of being able to experience the release of a technique as opposed to the planned execution of a technique.

Another common aspect of ranking is the individualization of the techniques at some higher grade, generally at the conferral of teaching certification. The actual grade held is essentially irrelevant outside the organizational structure.

Any visitor to a *dojo* will quickly reveal their relative ability in the first 10 minutes of training, and the actual belt worn can be ignored.

12.5 Training

The effect of the philosophical and ethical basis of one's martial art has already been referred to in the Introduction in terms of trophy hunting.

An additional aspect in the Japanese arts that is usually referred to (and glossed over) is Zen. Sometimes mixed up with this is the concept of *ki*.

One can get into difficult areas here (see the next section), but the effect of the Zen concepts on the training style is relatively simple to understand: It consists of cultivating an egoless patience with one's progress.

In terms of rank progression, before the rank test, the test is very important, but after the test is over, it is very unimportant. The goal is not to wear a particular color of cloth around the waist, but to improve the skill. Specifically, if a person is working on a particular problem in their technique on the day before a test, it is almost certain that they will be working an the same problem on the day after the test, regardless of the outcome of the test.

A Zen analogy is that of a bamboo leaf in a snow shower—it accumulates snow slowly and patiently, and when ready, slips free. In the same manner, one must accumulate training without attempting to hurry until the accumulated training can be transcended and one moves freely and naturally. Another analogy is that of measuring the height of a normally growing youth on a particular day. If the youth has not attained the height of, say, five feet, that youth has not "failed" this test of height in any real sense; growth will continue and the height will eventually be attained.

More importantly, students must be encouraged not to dwell on mistakes. If a mistake is made, no time should be wasted agonizing or even thinking about it other than noting that it occurred—the error is simply corrected on the next repetition of the situation or exercise. There will be several hundreds if not thousands of opportunities to correct each error during the succeeding years of training, after all. Have the students dwell on successes, and these will multiply. If the students dwell on what went wrong, their errors will become even more difficult to correct.

Additionally, just as the bamboo leaf does not tell the snow where and how much to deposit, so too the student should not tell the teacher how or what to teach, but realize that everything taught will be useful in its own way and in its own time (presupposing an enlightened and unselfish teacher). Rank will come automatically. This does not preclude thinking about or questioning each lesson, which is an integral part of realizing one's art, but it does preclude stubborn rejection and laziness, and in this manner emphasizes that the goal of a martial art is the perfection of character rather than simply learning to kill.

The classical teacher of *karate-do* does not teach a student how to punch, but rather how not to not punch. In other words, the process is not one of constant accretion of details, but rather of constant pruning of nonessentials, constant simplification and purification, until what remains is the flow of the *Tao* expressed as perfect punching that happens to be student-shaped.

It is this emphasis in training that differentiates *karate-do* (the spirit-way of the empty hand) from *shiai-jutsu* (tournament technique) or even *goshin-jutsu* (self-defense technique).

Chapter 13
Psychological Balance

How an individual interacts with the environment and especially with other people depends on that person's mental state during the process. Intense emotions like anger or fear can cloud the mind and prevent the free determination and selection of alternative paths of action.

Additionally, if a person has the need to completely and verbally preplan actions, this requirement inevitably will result in slowed responses to unexpected events. Verbal preplanning (e.g., "First I'll do this, then they'll do that, and I'll counter with...") without speaking aloud is called subvocalizing, and is an unconscious habit with many people.

This is related to a fundamental drive of the Western industrial mind, that of serialization (putting things in a neat single row) and narratization (explicitly telling a story) of all action. The Western mentality has been programmed by education and social convention into thinking the way a digital computer works—do one operation at a time after thinking it through first. Children are criticized in school when they impulsively try to do too many things at the same time, resulting in an appearance of chaotic disorder in which nothing seems to be accomplished.

Simultaneity or parallelism becomes impossible (a computer can't do two things at once).

In a reactive self-defense situation, this is suicide because a defender will always be "behind" the opponent in tempo since the attacker is already one step ahead, having initiated the interaction.

Alternatives exist to this serial way of thinking, although in many cultures, these alternatives often have been restricted to shamans, priests, or ascetics and occasionally are labeled as yogic, esoteric, or even magical practices.

Common to most if not all of the techniques of such altered thinking is an underlying assumption that the self or ego is either an illusion or at best a very incomplete description of reality. To combat this illusion, the most common method used in almost all of these philosophies involves some form of meditation in order to bypass the everyday mind and reveal an alternate form of both being and perceiving that does not depend on words.

Both the form and the results of attaining this experience differ depending on the cultural context. In some cases, it produces spiritual guides to the supernatural and/or divine (priests, shamans, and so on); elsewhere it is considered an essential step in order to become fully "real" and thus freed from the perception of a separate existence (yogic union with the Divine, Zen enlightenment).

In the specific case of the Japanese martial arts, bypassing the everyday mind and perceiving an alternate form of being is the defining step that makes an individual a true master of the art rather than simply a very experienced technician. Therefore, both meditation and perception exercises are considered indispensable to martial arts practice since self-defense responses must be made instantaneously and spontaneously.

In the Zen Buddhist literature attached to the modern Japanese martial arts (especially kendo and kyudo—swordsmanship and archery), much is made of the necessity for this experience of a different reality to occur before an individual can become truly competent, avoiding both verbal preplanning and emotional turmoil.

In kyudo, practice is geared toward allowing "it" to shoot, that is, to keep the verbally worrying ego self completely inactive during the process. The assumption is that with such internal quiet, there will be no disturbance of the shooting and thus no mistakes or possibly fatal misses. This psychological equanimity and inherent mental and physical balance is the main focus of modern kyudo practice.

In kendo, the same ideas are expressed: The process of planning distracts from the process of doing, and results in being killed. Additionally, the fear of being killed results not in self-preservation, but in death. True technique is said to arise "from the Void" as a marvelous unfolding of not-doing (in a Taoist sense), and not from the discursive, ego-bound mind of the individual.

Modern karate-do has also absorbed some of this attitude and has adopted much of the swordsmanship literature and its parables as a model of how it is to conduct its own mental training.

Japanese karate-do uses two terms taken from Zen Buddhism to describe aspects of the mental state necessary to produce proper responses: "Mind like the moon" (*tsuki-no-kokoro*) and "mind like water" (*mizu-no-kokoro*). This implies that the mind should be placid and calm, but quick as light, just as the moon loses no time producing its reflection in still water.

The image is poetic and has been used to indicate the immediacy with which an enlightened individual experiences the world.

While the analogy of the moon reflected in a calm pond is excellent, it does not provide us with an explicit set of training techniques designed to get us to this state. Partly, this is because the phrase was invented by Buddhist philosophers who probably already were enlightened, and partly because it seems to be a description of an effect felt when proper responding was occurring rather than a means to cause such responses.

In other words, when one looked back at a successful response, the state of mind associated with it was remembered, but there apparently was no way to get to it ahead of time, and no way to train directly for it either, except through meditation. Naturally, all this supposes that one has a technical foundation already attained in order to provide the appropriate tools to the Void for expression, but such technical training alone cannot gain access to the Void. On the other hand, Zen enlightenment without technical training will allow one to die with equanimity and full awareness, but without being able to effectively defend oneself, which is not a particularly useful goal for the karate-ka.

How is the prosaic Western mind to gain access to what seems to be a relatively closed and somewhat self-referential philosophy apparently at odds with everyday experience?

One method is to invoke cognitive psychology and restate both the underlying differentiation of the ego from the "true Self" and the associated process of enlightenment in different terms. The differentiation of the planning ego from the "true Self" can be thought of as being defined by the same split in ways of perceiving as the left brain/right brain dichotomy in cognitive psychology.

Much of the scientific data that underlies this analysis comes from patients whose cerebral hemispheres have been surgically split, usually to relieve intractable epilepsy, and from patients who have survived with local brain injury. In conjunction with the surgical split of the brain in the epilepsy patients, there is also a split in the visual field in that things shown to one side of the center of vision go only to the opposite side of the brain, and vice versa, thus allowing specific testing of each hemisphere separately and simultaneously. What these individuals show is that each brain hemisphere can process information independently and completely, although with certain differing abilities depending on the task.

Adding in the data from the injury patients, it seems that in general (somewhat simplistically and with the split overstated), the left brain is optimized to process information serially, e.g., language, numbers, time scheduling, and so on, while the right brain is better at processing items in parallel or as patterns, e.g., pictures, faces, contexts, music, and so on.

The implication then is that the verbal ego actually is predominantly a function of the left hemisphere. This idea is supported by research that shows severe language deficits with left brain damage (specifically temporal lobe), but almost undetectable changes if the same areas are damaged in the right hemisphere. Finally, there is some data which indicates that in the intact brain, the left language areas actually inhibit the equivalent areas on the right hemisphere.

With this underpinning of neurophysiology, at least some of the meditative techniques begin to make more sense. Mantra yoga (the recurrent internal chanting of a set of syllables) can be seen to be essentially hypnotizing the left brain verbal centers to "free" the right brain areas from domination or inhibition. The Zen *koan* system of puzzles with no verbal or logical solution can be conceived of as attempting to maximally overload and frustrate this same way of thinking, again with the goal of empowering an alternate way of thinking.

The martial arts method of training an individual into exhaustion so that the student is, in essence, too tired to think, but still must respond is another method to short-circuit the verbal habits and release control to something that is not verbal—the right brain.

Based on this type of analysis, a set of experiences can be sought that not only allows an individual to experience and validate the idea of a non-verbal, non-ego way of thinking, but also actively to train in such a manner as to encourage its emergence. Such training may be an over-correction in that it attempts to completely suppress the left brain verbal functioning, but it is needed since the overwhelming requirement of day-to-day modern living is dependent almost exclusively on use of the verbal ego.

In my personal experience, one can perceive the world with either hemisphere dominant. The internal feeling of the two ways of seeing is very different: When the left brain is the primary seat of activity, one has a strong sense of "I," and there is a feeling of a measured linear flow to time; sequential analysis of individual details is the way one deals with any presented information. On the other hand, right-brain thinking is a less common experience. In such a state, the "I" becomes passive and verbally silent (such as can happen when staring into a fire or listening with the eyes closed to multi-harmonic line music), the time sense is suspended or at least irrelevant, and the relationships between things rather than the things themselves are perceived more clearly.

The body itself also feels very different: While the left brain is in control, one actively is moving the individual parts of one's body. When the right brain is allowed to take over, the parts themselves seem to be doing the moving without a centralized controller. The verbal "I" as a left brain construct is simply an impartial and relatively silent witness that appears to stand apart or "outside" the action.

The way to apply this idea to training is relatively easy to state, albeit more difficult in practice. In karate-do, the actual learning of new techniques is handled by the left brain; the practice or performance of the art is under right brain control.

Also, one can only practice that which one has learned. In order to succeed in a fight, one cannot act as if one were training in the *dojo*. The entire pattern of the opponent must be grasped and the response pattern (which will involve a set of parallel sequences happening simultaneously) must be initiated instantaneously. This can only happen efficiently if the individual in not preplanning each move, i.e., has inhibited the left brain and is thinking predominantly with the right brain. With this transition in the way of thinking, the "I" being attacked seems to disappear, the opponent as a separate entity disappears, and only the linked space in between really exists. This results in the sought after absence of fear and it results in the clear vision needed to freely perform the techniques previously learned.

In the *dojo*, the occasional experience of the perfect counterattack during free sparring, (which felt so absolutely effortless that it generated the question afterwards of "where did that come from?") is an example of what can happen when left brain thinking gets out of the way. The opponent perceives only that an attack arrived from nowhere that gave him no time to counter.

This state (perfect technique) is in fact a Zen state of "enlightenment" (*kensho*), however transient. This same left to right brain shift can be seen in any of a dozen *kensho* poems in the Zen literature, both inside and outside of the martial arts, and such poems should be studied for hints on how to recognize it.

13.1 Training Methods

To approach this mental balance point, various exercises are useful.

For the eyes, simply walking in open areas with the gaze fixed on the horizon will still the mental dialogue and increase concentration as well as sensitivity in the peripheral visual fields to avoid tripping over obstacles below the gaze.

Climbing and descending stairs without looking down helps development of both mental and physical equilibrium.

Meditation—sitting and simply listening—will open the mind to outside stimuli normally masked by the internal racket.

Finally, breathing exercises utilizing both visualization of "paths" (i.e., in the nose, through the skull, down the spine, under and up into the *hara*, up and out of the mouth) as well as timing (in-breath in four heartbeats, out-breath in four heartbeats; then later, in with four, held with four, out with four, held with four) will help. Concentrating on the breathing in *kata* practice also will help develop a strong and immovable center. The point of such breathing exercises is to develop control, timing, and sensitivity. Breathing exercises are a means, not an end in themselves.

Training in the *dojo* can help make the transition from thinking to doing. One of the classical methods is doing one *kata* continuously for an hour without stopping. One of the basic forms is best for this because it does not require much remembering.

More dynamic training can be done in attack/defense drills with "bull in the ring" exercises. The defender is placed in the center of a ring of six to eight students; each may attack at will, even from behind, provided a trigger (a stamp or a *kiai*) is given before the attack.

Alternatively, the person in the center can be given a wooden sword and may without warning strike down at any member of the circle, who must then intercept the blow by moving into and under it and across to the opposite side of the circle.

Both of these exercises can only be successfully completed if the mind is clear and quiet. As soon as an individual starts to think verbally and attempt to pre-plan or anticipate the attack, the reaction times will become too long and the person will be struck.

It must not be thought that this state of mind implies slowness or a loss of fighting spirit. On the contrary, the individual's will is freed from vacillation and the difference between free sparring and actual fighting is established via *san-bun dome* ("3/10 of a cm stopping") or *sun-dome* ("one-inch stopping"), as well as the freely accepted restrictions of techniques to be used. These rules do not interfere with the right brain's control of the execution of the techniques; merely the verbalization is cleared away from the actual doing.

An initial approach to this state is the earlier mentioned concept of *ai-uchi*, or mutual striking, and is best taught at the brown belt stage of development. With this concept, if a defender sees or feels an attack coming, the correct response is to ignore the attack itself and simply attack the attacker faster and harder with the intent to pre-empt the focus, letting the defensive moves arise spontaneously. Western folklore reflects this idea in the concepts of "taking an honor guard to Hell" or in the mentality of the old Norse berserker. The underlying assumption is that the person in the interchange with the least amount of double-mindedness will have the swiftest techniques and the least hesitation, thus winning what was set up as a mutual kill situation.

A standard practice for this is called "the slaughterline." A defender is placed with the back heel in stance against a wall, preventing any retreat. The other members of the class line up in single file facing the defender and sequentially and as quickly as possible execute a stepping attack (initially stepping punch), then get out of the way of the next attacker, moving to the back of the line. In order to survive, the defender must attack the attacker's technique as soon as it begins to move, even though a purely pre-emptive counterattack is forbidden in the exercise.

This ability to turn off the internal dialogue and let the training one has absorbed express itself egolessly, i.e., to experience the "death" of the "I," in a high tension situation where the "I" is most threatened, such as free sparring in a tournament, is the critical difference and the mark of the qualitative change between a beginning student and a beginning teacher. Ideally, this should be marked by the change from *kyu* to *dan* ranks, but the exact rank at which experiencing this shift is required can vary between schools.

Nevertheless, one must have the experience of shifting consciously into the right brain mode at least once to graduate into the higher level of understanding.

When this becomes the normal pattern of thought, the person no longer can be caught by surprise and may be called a "master."

This is the meaning of the statement that one (the ego) must die at least once before one (the "true Self" harmonized with the ego) realizes the martial art.

In Zen, this setting aside of a separate ego state, with the resulting unification of individual inside the skin with the world outside the skin into one perceptive reality is termed *kensho*. Only after this apparent death can one have true practice of the martial art as opposed to simply training in martial techniques.

Then, if one is so unfortunate as to have to fight, one merely "practices" one's art without selfish intent for ego gratification, and the opponent, in effect, commits suicide.

Appendix A
Bibliography

The references given here have formed part of the foundation of my thinking on training, and also include my books on *kata* analysis and application. In some of them, you will find sections that echo what I have written; in others, a complementary expression of ideas. I believe that these few books can form a reference nucleus for the martial arts instructor who wishes to go beyond both trophy hunting and homicide. They form part of a matrix of information from which one might develop a personal path toward "mastership."

Budden P., *Looking at a Far Mountain—A Study of Kendo Kata*. Charles E. Tuttle Co., Rutland, VT (2000).

Draeger, D. F. *The Martial Arts and Ways of Japan*, Vols 1-3. Weatherhill, New York, NY (1973).

Egami, S. *The Way of Karate Beyond Technique*. Kodansha International, San Francisco, CA (1976).

Ingber, L. *The Karate Instructor's Handbook*. Institute for the Study of Attention, Solana Beach, CA (1976).

Inosanto, D. *Jeet Kune Do / The Art and Philosophy of Bruce Lee*. Know Now Publishing Company, Los Angeles, CA (1980).

Jaynes, J. *The Origin of Consciousness in the Breakdown of the Bicameral Mind*. Houghton Mifflin Co., Boston, MA (1982).

Koyama, S. *Karate and Health*. Privately published (1980).

Liang, T. T. *T'ai Chi Ch'uan for Health and Self-defense/Philosophy and Practice*. (Vintage Books) Random House, New York, NY (1974).

Miyamoto, M. *A Book of Five Rings* tr. V. Harris. Overlook Press, Woodstock NY (1974).

Nakayama, M. *Dynamic Karate*. Kodansha International, Palo Alto, CA (1966).

Ratti, O., and Westbrook, A. *Secrets of the Samurai*. Charles E. Tuttle Co., Rutland, VT (1973).

Schmeisser, E. T. *Bunkai: Secrets of Karate Kata Vol 1: The Tekki Series*. Tamashii Press, St. Louis, MO (2000)

Schmeisser, E. T. Channan - *The Heart of the Heians*. Usagi Press Japan, Kanazawa, Japan (2004)

Suzuki, D. T. *Zen and Japanese Culture*. Bollingen Series LXIV, Princeton University Press, Princeton, NJ (1970).

Westbrook, A., and Ratti, O. *Aikido and the Dynamic Sphere*. Charles E. Tuttle Co., Rutland, VT (1970).

Note:
Appendix C (Glossary) was derived from information shared on the Karate Cyber-Dojo, an international computer network for people who train in traditional Japanese/Okinawan karate systems.

For information, contact Howard High, Network Administrator, by e-mail: high@jkr.com; or at Japan Karate-Do Ryobu-Kai, 5145 Buena Vista Dr., Roeland Park, KS 66205, USA (913) 384-9416 or (913) 384-5890.

Appendix B
Dojo Etiquette

The following description is given as an example of the formalities normally associated with a traditional and highly formal Japanese-style JKA-Shotokan dojo.

In America, the opening of class can range from a simple standing bow between the teacher and the students to a level of ceremony that matches the most formal in Japan. Likewise, in modern day Japan, classes may simply begin and end with a mutual bow. It should be noted that the behavior surrounding karate classes has a rationale: Not only does it indicate that this period of time is special and outside of normal, day-to-day life, but just as a gold and pearl frame around an icon indicates the icon's worth, so do formal meditation and bowing procedures indicate the students' and teachers' reverence not only for what is being learned, but also for its historical context.

Dojo Etiquette

1. Upon entering the *dojo*, one bows to the *kamiza* ("high place") of the *dojo*, generally the front. This place may have an alcove with a scroll or a picture in it. In some dojo, it may even have a small Shinto style shrine (*kamiza*).

2. The dojo *sempai* (usually the senior *kyu* student), upon a signal from the *sensei* (teacher), calls for the lineup, in order of rank, with the highest rank on the right, facing forward. If multiple rows are needed, they continue in order from upper to lower behind the first row. The *dai-sempai* ("number-one elder brother": usually *dan* grade students) may line up on the right, facing in, with the highest grade closest to the front. (Note: Some *dojos* do not have a separate line for the black belt students). Other dojo may not use the term "*sempai*" at all; however, in America, it has become somewhat common, even though it does not match Japanese usage.

3. After the lineup is complete, the *sempai* calls "*kiotsuke*" (attention), after which the *sensei* steps onto the *dojo* floor and kneels down in

front of the class facing the (occasionally virtual) *kamiza*. If there is an assistant *sensei*, he follows onto the floor, goes to his place, and kneels down. The *dai-sempai* then also kneel down.

```
                        KAMIZA

                        Sensei
                          X

Assistant Sensei   X


                                      X   Dai Sempai
                                      X
                                      X

OOOOOOOOOOOOOOOOOOOOOOOX Sempai
            Class
```

4. The *sempai* calls "*seiza*" (sit) and the line of junior students quickly kneels in order of rank.

5. The *sempai* calls "*mokuso*" (meditate or concentrate); silence with lowered eyes and calmed breathing is maintained for about a minute.

6. The *sempai* calls "*mokuso yame*" (meditate-ending-ready). If this is the end of class, *Dojo Kun* may follow, q.v.

7. The *sempai* calls "*shomen-ni-rei*" (to the front, bow); all bow to show respect to the founders of the art (silently).

8. The *sensei* will turn around clockwise on his knees and face the class, whereupon the *sempai* calls "*sensei-ni-rei*" (to the teacher, bow); the

class and the teacher bow to each other, the class requesting instruction if this is the beginning of class by saying "*onegai-shimasu*" (essentially "please"). If this is the end of class, the students say "*arigato-gozai-mashita*" (thank you).

9. The *sempai* then calls "*otagai-ni-rei*" (to each other, bow); all the students bow showing respect to each other for training together. Depending on the dojo, the *sensei* may not bow to the students, as this is not really directed to him; alternatively, he may bow, recognizing that he is a fellow student. However, he will exchange bows with any assistant *sensei* or honored guests and in some *dojo*, with the *dai-sempai*.

10. If this is the beginning of class, the *sensei* rises and the class begins here. If it is the end, the *sensei* rises and bows off the floor, and the following courtesies may be followed.

11. If there are *dai-sempai*, the *sempai* calls "*sempai-ni-rei*" (to the elder, bow), whereupon they exchange bows.

12. The *dai-sempai* rise and bow off the floor.

13. The students then bow silently again to the *kamiza* and get up to leave the floor in order of rank.

B.1   Dojo Kun

Dojo Kun
(*Dojo* Precepts)

Hitotsu! Jinkaku kansei ni tsutomeru koto!
(Point! Seek completion of character!)

Hitotsu! Makato no michi o mamoru koto!
(Point! Protect sincerity!)

Hitotsu! Doryoku no seishin o yashinao koto!
(Point! Build strong spirit!)

Hitotsu! Reigi o omonjiru koto!
(Point! Show good manners!)

Hitotsu! Kekki no yu o imashimeru koto!
(Point! Avoid reckless behavior!)

Ijo!
(So be it!)

Each line of the *Dojo Kun* is spoken first by the *sempai*, and then repeated (generally rather forcefully) by the class; the initial *"Dojo Kun"* and the concluding *"Ijo"* is spoken only by the *sempai*. Depending on the *dojo*, they can be spoken in either English or Japanese, and the translations may vary, often widely since the Japanese words contain a much wider set of meanings than the simple English phrases really can convey.

Appendix C
Glossary

The following Japanese glossary of terms was compiled through the contributions of several martial artists on an electronic computer bulletin board managed by Howard High at the University of Kansas. It is one of the most complete I have seen, and their help is gratefully acknowledged. They are: Dave Bockus, Brad Cahoon, Sam Weaver, Howard High, Denise Kask, Maryellen Read, Kevin Picott, and Steve Popovich. (See Bibliography for more information.)

The pronunciation guide is American rather than European. If it makes no sense, ignore it in favor of European vowel values, remembering to pronounce each vowel separately (no dipthongs).

Blocks

Age-uke	(ah-geh oo-kay)	Rising block
Age-uke gyaku ashi	(ah-geh oo-kay gya-koo ah-she)	Up block (reverse foot)
Ashibo-kake-uke	(ah-she-boh kah-keh oo-kay)	Leg hooking block
Ashikubi-kake-uke	(ah-she-koo-be kah-keh-oo-kay)	Ankle hooking block
Awase-uke	(ah-wah-say oo-kay)	Joined hand block
Cho-cho-uke	(choe-choe oo-kay)	Butterfly block
Chudan-shuto-uke	(chew-dahn shoe-toe oo-kay)	Knife hand block against body attack
Chudan-uchi-uke	(chew-dahn oo-chee oo-kay)	Forearm block outward from inside
Chudan-ude-uke	(chew-dahn oo-deh oo-kay)	Forearm block against body attack
Chudan-uke	(chew-dahn oo-kay)	Middle blocks in general
Deai-osae-uke	(deh-aye oh-sah-eh oo-kay)	Pressing block while stepping in

Fumikomi-age-uke	(foo-me-ko-me ah-geh oo-kay)	Up block stepping in
Fumikomi-shuto-uke	(foo-me-ko-me shoe-toe oo-kay)	Knife hand block stepping in
Fumikomi-ude-uke	(foo-me-ko-me oo-deh oo-kay)	Forearm block while stepping in
Gedan-barai	(geh-dahn bah-rye)	Low level block
Gedan-kake-uke	(geh-dahn kah-keh oo-kay)	Low level hooking block
Gedan-uke	(geh-dahn oo-kay)	Low level block
Gedan-ude-uke	(geh-dahn oo-day oo-kay)	Low forearm block
Haishu-uke	(hi-shoo oo-kay)	Backhand block
Haiwan-nagashi-uke	(ha-ee-wahn nah-gah-she oo-kay)	Back-arm sweeping block
Haiwan-uke	(hi-wahn oo-kay)	Upper forearm block
Hiji-suri-uke	(he-jee sue-rhee oo-kay)	Elbow sliding block
Hiji-uke	(he-jee oo-kay)	Elbow block
Hiki-uke	(hee-key oo-kay)	Pulling/grasping block
Hiza-uke	(he-zah oo-kay)	Knee block
Jodan-age-uke	(joe-dahn ah- geh oo-kay)	Upper block against head attack
Jodan-uke	(joe-dahn oo-kay)	Upper block in general
Juji-uke	(jew-jee oo-kay)	X-block
Kake-shuto-uke	(kah-kay shoe- toe oo-kay)	Hooking knife hand block
Kake-uke	(kay-kay oo-kay)	Hooking block
Kakiwake-uke	(kah-key-wah- kay oo-kay)	Reverse wedge block
Kakuto-uke	(kah-kuh-toe oo-kay)	Bent-wrist block
Keito-uke	(kay-toe oo-kay)	Chicken-head wrist block
Ko-uke	(koh oo-kay)	Wrist block, Arch block
Maeude-deai-osae	(mah-eh oo-deh deh-aye oh-saheh)	Forearm pressing block
Maeude-hineri-uke	(mah-eh-oo-deh he-neh-rhee oo-kay)	Forearm twist block
Mawashi-uke	(mah-wha-shee oo-kay)	Roundhouse block
Morote-sukui-uke	(moh-row-teh sue-koo-ee oo-kay)	Two-handed scooping block

Morote-tsukami-uke	(moh-row-teh tsue-kah-me oo-kay)	Two-handed grasping block
Morote-uke	(moe-row-teh oo-kay)	Augmented forearm block
Nagashi-uke	(nah-gah-she oo-kay)	Sweeping block
Oroshi-uke	(oh-roe-shee oo-kay)	Descending block
Osae-uke	(oh-sah-eh oo-keh)	Pressing block
Otoshi-uke	(oh-toe-she oo-kay)	Dropping block
Sashite-uke	(sah-she-tay oo-kay)	Rising hand block
Seiryuto-uke	(say-ryu-toh oo-kay)	Ox-jaw block
Shotei-uke	(show-tay oo-kay)	Palm heel block
Shuto-uke	(shoe-toe oo-kay)	Knife hand block
Sokumen-awase-uke	(so-koo-men ah-wah-say oo-kay)	Side two-hand block
Sokutei-mawashi-uke	(so-koo-tay mah-wah-she oo-kay)	Circular sole block
Sokutei-osae-uke	(so-koo-tay oh-sah-eh oo-kay)	Pressing block with sole of foot
Sokuto-osae-uke	(so-koo-to oh-sah-eh oo-kay)	Pressing block with foot edge
Soto-uke	(so-toh oo-kay)	Block from outside inward
Sukui-uke	(sue-koo-ee oo-kay)	Scooping block
Tate-shuto-uke	(tah-teh shoe-toe oo-kay)	Vertical knife hand block
Tate-uke	(tah-teh oo-kay)	Vertical block
Te-nagashi-uke	(teh na-gah-she oo-kay)	Hand sweeping block
Te-osae-uke	(teh oh-sah-eh oo-kay)	Hand pressing block
Teisho-awase-uke	(tay-show ah-wah-say oo-kay)	Combined palm-heel block
Teisho-uke	(tay-sho oo-kay)	Palm-heel block
Tekubi-kake-uke	(teh-koo-be kah-kay oo-kay)	Wrist-hook block
Tettsui uke	(tet-soo-ee oo-keh)	Hammer fist block
Tsukami-uke	(tsue-kah-me oo-kay)	Grasping block
Uchi-uke	(oo-chee oo-kay)	Block from inside outward
Ude-uke	(oo-day oo-kay)	Forearm block
Uke	(oo-kay)	Blocking

Punches

Age-zuki	(ah-geh zoo-key)	Rising punch
Awase-zuki	(ah-wah-say zoo-key)	U – punch
Choku-zuki	(cho-koo zoo-key)	Straight punch
Chudan-choku-zuki	(chew-dahn cho-koo zoo-key)	Straight punch to body
Chudan-zuki	(chew-dahn zoo-key)	Middle area punch
Dan-zuki	(dahn zoo-key)	Consecutive punching
Furi-zuki	(foo-ree zoo-key)	Circular punch
Gedan-choku-zuki	(geh-dahn cho-koo zoo-key)	Straight punch to low area
Gedan-zuki	(geh-dahn zoo-key)	Punch to low area
Gyaku-zuki	(gya-koo zoo-key)	Reverse punch
Hasami-zuki	(hah-sah-me zoo-key)	Scissors punch
Heiko-zuki	(Hay-koh zoo-key)	Double punch, simultaneous
Hiraken-zuki	(he-rah-ken zoo-key)	Fore-knuckle-fist straight punch
Hon-zuki	(hohn zoo-key)	Frontal punch
Ippon-ken zuki	(eep-pone ken zoo-key)	One-knuckle-fist straight punch
Jodan-choku-zuki	(joe-dahn cho-koo zoo-key)	Upper straight punch
Jodan-zuki	(joe-dahn zoo-key)	Upper punch
Jun-zuki	(joon zoo-key)	Jab punch
Kagi-zuki	(kah-ghee zoo-key)	Hook punch
Kizami-zuki	(key-zah-me zoo-key)	Jab
Mae-ken-zuki	(mah-eh-ken zoo-key)	Lead hand punch
Maete	(mah-eh-te)	Jab
Mawashi-zuki	(mah-wha-she zoo-key)	Roundhouse punch
Morote-zuki	(moe-row-teh zoo-key)	Double-fist "U" punch
Nagashi-zuki	(nah-gah-she zoo-key)	Flowing punch
Nihon-zuki	(nee-hohn zoo-key)	Double punch

Oi-zuki	(oh-ee zoo-key)	Lunge punch
Oroshi-zuki	(oh-roe-shee zoo-key)	Descending punch
Renzuki	(wren-zoo-key)	Alternate punching
Ryusui-zuki	(ree-oo-soo-ee zoo-key)	Flowing punch
Sanbon-zuki	(san-bohn zoo-key)	Three punch combination
Sanren-zuki	(san-wren zoo-key)	Three consecutive punches
Seiken-choku-zuki	(say-ken cho-koo zoo-key)	Fore-fist straight punch
Seiken-zuki	(say-ken zoo-key)	Forefist middle thrust
Tate-zuki	(tah-teh zoo-key)	Vertical fist punch
Teisho-zuki	(tay-show zoo-key)	Palm-heel punch
Tsuki	(tsue-key)	Punching
Tsuki-waza	(tsue-key wah-zah)	Punching techniques
Ura-zuki	(oo-rah zoo-key)	Close range uppercut punch
Yama-zuki	(yah-mah zoo-key)	Mountain punch
Yoko-zuki	(yoh-koh zoo-key)	Side punch

Kicks

Ago geri	(ah-go geh-rhee)	Chin kick
Ashi-Barai	(ah-she bah-rye)	Foot sweep
Chudan-mae-geri	(chew-dahn mah-eh geh-rhee)	Front kick to body
En-sho	(en-show)	Round heel
Fumikiri	(foo-me-key-rhee)	Cutting kick
Fumikomi	(foo-me-koh-me)	Stamping kick
Gedan-kekomi	(geh-dahn kay-koh-me)	Thrust kick to low target level
Gyaku-ashi	(gya-koo ah-she)	Reverse foot
Gyaku-geri	(gya-koo geh-rhee)	Reversed kick
Gyaku-mawashi-geri	(gya-koo mah-wah-she geh-rhee)	Reverse round kick

Hiza-geri	(he-zah geh-rhee)	Knee kick
Jodan-kekomi	(joe-dahn kay-koh-me)	Thrust kick to face
Jodan-mae-geri	(joe-dahn mah-eh geh-rhee)	Front kick to face
Keage	(key-ah-geh)	Snap kick
Kebanashi	(kay-bah-nah-she)	Kick off (snap kick)
Kekomi	(kay-koh-me)	Thrust kick
Kensetsu-geri	(ken-set-sue geh-rhee)	Stamping kick, or joint kick
Keri	(kay-rhee)	Kicking
Keri ashi	(keh-rhee ash-ee)	Kicking foot
Keri-waza	(kay-rhee wha-zah)	Kicking techniques
Kesa-geri	(keh-sah geh-rhee)	Diagonal kick
Kin-geri	(kin geh-rhee)	Groin kick
Mae-ashi-geri	(mah-eh ah-she geh-rhee)	Front leg kick
Mae-ashi kekomi	(mah-ee-ah-shee keh-koh-mee)	Front leg thrust
Mae-geri	(mah-eh geh-rhee)	Front kick
Mae-geri-keage	(mah-eh geh-rhee kay-ah-geh)	Front snap kick
Mae-geri-kekomi	(mah-eh geh-rhee kay-koh-me)	Front thrust kick
Mae-tobi-geri	(mah-eh toe-be geh-rhee)	Jumping front kick
Mawashi-geri	(mah-wha-she geh-rhee)	Round kick
Mikazuki-geri	(me-kah-zoo-key geh-rhee)	Crescent kick
Nidan-geri	(nee-dahn geh-rhee)	Double jump kick
Renzoku-geri	(wren-zoe-koo geh-rhee)	Combination kick
Sokuto	(soh-koo-toe)	Edge of foot
Sokuto Keage	(soh-koo-toe kay ah-geh)	Snap kick with foot edge
Tobi-geri	(toh-bee-geh-ree)	Flying front kick
Tobi-yoko-geri	(toh-be yoh-koh-geh-rhee)	Jumping side kick
Uchi-mawashi-geri	(oo-chee mah-wah-she geh-rhee)	Inside roundhouse kick
Ushiro-ashi-geri	(oo-she-roh ah-she geh-rhee)	Rear-leg kick
Ushiro-geri	(oo-she-roh geh-rhee)	Back kick

Yoko-geri	(yoh-koh geh-rhee)	Side kick
Yoko-geri-keage	(yoh-koh geh-rhee keh-ah-geh)	Side snap kick
Yoko-geri-kekomi	(yoh-koh geh-rhee keh-koh-me)	Side thrust kick
Yoko-kekomi	(yoh-koh keh-koh-me)	Side thrust kick
Yoko-tobi-geri	(yoh-koh toe-be geh-rhee)	Jumping side kick

Others

Atama-uchi	(ah-tahm-ah oo-chee)	Strike with head
Ate-waza	(ah-teh wah-zah)	Smashing techniques
Empi	(em-pee)	Elbow
Empi-uchi	(em-pee oo-chee)	Elbow Strike
Enpi	(en-pee)	Elbow attacks
Ganmen uchi	(gan-men oo-chee)	Facial strike
Hai-wan	(ha-ee wahn)	Back-arm
Haishu-uchi	(hah-ee-shoo oo-chee)	Backhand strike
Haito	(hah-ee-toh)	Ridge hand
Haito-uchi	(hah-ee-toh oo-chee)	Ridge-hand strike
Heiwan-uchi	(hah-ee-wahn oo-chee)	Forearm strike
Hiji-ate	(he-jee ah-teh)	Elbow smash
Hiji-atemi	(he-jee ah-teh-me)	Elbow strikes
Hiji-uchi	(he-jee oo-chee)	Elbow strike
Hiraken	(he-rah-ken)	Fore-knuckle fist
Hitosashi-ippon-ken	(hih-toh-sah-she ee-pohn ken)	Forefinger knuckle
Hizagashira	(he-zah-gah-she-rah)	Knee cap
Hiza-uchi	(he-zah oo-chee)	Knee strike
Ippon-ken	(eep-pone ken)	One-knuckle fist
Ippon-nukite	(eep-pone noo-key-teh)	Stabbing action with forefinger extended
Kentsui	(ken-tsue-ee)	Hammer fist
Kentsui-uchi	(ken-tsue-ee oo-chee)	Fist-hammer strike
Ko-uchi	(koh-oo-chee)	Bent wrist strike
Kumade	(koo-mah-deh)	Bear-hand
Mae-empi-uchi	(mah-eh en-pee oo-chee)	Forward elbow strike
Mae-hiji-ate	(mah-eh he-jee ah-teh)	Forward elbow smash

Mawashi-hiji-ate	(mah-wah-she he-jee ah-teh)	Circular elbow smash
Nakadaka-ippon-ken	(nah-kah-dah-kah-eep-pone-ken)	Middle finger one-knuckle fist
Nakadaka-ken	(nah-kah-dah-kah-ken)	Middle-finger knuckle fist
Nihon-nukite	(nee-hone-noo-key-teh)	Two finger spear-hand
Nukite	(noo-key-teh)	Spear-hand
Otoshi-empi-uchi	(oh-toe-she en-pee oo-chee)	Downward elbow strike
Otoshi-hiji-ate	(oh-toe-she he-jee ah-teh)	Downward elbow smash
Oyayubi-ippon-ken	(oh-yah-you-bee-eep-pohn ken)	Thumb knuckle fist
Sashite	(sah-she-tay)	Raising hand to strike
Seiryuto	(say-ryu-toh)	Ox-jaw hand
Shittsui	(shit-tsue-ee)	Knee-hammer
Shu-wan	(shoe-wahn)	Palm arm
Shubo	(shoe-boh)	Arm-stick
Shuto	(shoe-toe)	Knife hand
Shuto-uchi	(shoe-toe oo-chee)	Knife hand strike
Sokuto	(soh-koo-toe)	Foot edge
Tate-empi-uchi	(tah-teh en-pee oo-chee)	Upward elbow strike
Tate-hiji-ate	(tah-teh he-jee ah-teh)	Upward elbow smash
Teisho	(tay-show)	Palm-heel
Teisho-uchi	(tay-show oo-chee)	Palm-heel strike
Tettsui	(tett-soo-ee)	Hammer fist
Tettsui-uchi	(tett-soo-ee oo-chee)	Bottom fist strike
Tsuki	(tsue-key)	Punch or thrust
Uchi	(oo-chee)	Striking
Uchi-waza	(oo-chee wah-zah)	Striking techniques
Ude	(oo-deh)	Forearm
Uraken	(oo-rah-ken)	Backfist
Uraken-uchi	(oo-rah-ken oo-chee)	Backfist strike
Ushiro-empi-uchi	(oo-she-row en-pee oo-chee)	Back elbow strike
Ushiro-hiji-ate	(oo-she-row he-jee ah-teh)	Back elbow smash
Wanto	(wahn-toe)	Arm sword
Washide	(wah-she-deh)	Eagle hand
Yoko-empi-uchi	(yoh-koh en-pee oo-chee)	Side elbow strike
Yoko-hiji-ate	(yoh-koh he-jee ah-teh)	Side elbow smash

Yoko-mawashi-empi-uchi	(yoh-koh mah-wah-she -een-pee oo-chee)	Side-round elbow strike
Yoko-mawashi-hiji-ate	(yoh-koh mah-wah-shee he-jee ah-teh)	Side-round elbow smash

Stances

Ayumi ashi	(a-yoo-me ash-ee)	Natural stepping
Fudo-dachi also *Sochin-dachi* (q.v.)	(foo-dough dah-chee)	Rooted stance
Gankaku-dachi also *Tsuri-ashi-dachi* and *Sagi-ashi-dachi* (q.v.)	(gahn-kah-koo dah-chee)	One legged stance
Gedan no kamae	(gay-dahn no kah-may)	Lower level combat posture
Hachiji-dachi	(hah-chee-jee dah-chee)	Open-leg stance
Hangetsu-dachi	(hahn-geh-tsue dah-chee)	Half-moon stance
Hanmi	(hahn-me)	Half-front facing
Hanmi no kamae	(han-me no kah-mah-ee)	Half-front facing posture
Han-zenkutsu-dachi	(hahn zen-koo-tsue dah-chee)	Half forward stance
Heiko-dachi	(hay-koh dah-chee)	Parallel stance
Heisoku-dachi	(hay-soh-koo dah-chee)	Informal attention stance
Hidari-shizen-tai	(he-dah-rhee she-zen tah-ee)	Left natural position
Hidari-teiji-dachi	(he-dah-rhee teh-ee-jee dah-chee)	Left T-stance
Jodan no kamae	(joh-dahn no kah-may)	Upper level combat posture
Kiba-dachi also *Naihanchin-dachi* or *Naifanchin-dachi* (q.v.)	(key-bah dah-chee)	Straddle-leg stance
Kokutsu-dachi	(koe-koo-tsu dah-chee)	Back stance
Kosa-dachi	(koe-sah dah-chee)	Crossed legged stance
Musubi-dachi	(moo-sue-be dah-chee)	Informal stance, feet turned out
Naifanchin-dachi also *Naihanchin-dachi* or *Kiba-Dachi* (q.v.)	(ni-fahn-chin dah-chee)	Straddle leg stance

Naihanshi-dachi	(ni-hahn-she dah-chee)	*Kiba-dachi* with knees turned in and down
Naihanchin-dachi also *Naifanchin-dachi* or *Kiba-Dachi* (q.v.)	(ni-hahn-chin dah-chee)	Straddle leg stance
Neko-ashi-dachi	(neh-koh ah-shedah-chee)	Cat stance
Reinoji-dachi	(ray-no-jee dah-chee)	L stance
Sagi-ashi-dachi also *Tsuri-ashi-dachi* or *Gankaku-ashi-dachi* (q.v.)	(sah-gee ah-shee dah-chee)	Propped stance
Sanchin-dachi	(san-chin dah-chee)	Hour-glass stance
Seisan-dachi	(seh-sahn dah-chee)	Side facing straddle stance
Shiko-dachi	(she-ko dah-chee)	Square stance
Shizen-dachi no kamae	(she-zen no kah-may)	Natural combat posture
Shizentai	(she-zen tay)	Natural position
Sochin-dachi also *Fudo-dachi* (q.v.)	(so-chin dah-chee)	Diagonal side stance
Suri ashi	(soo-rhee ash-ee)	Sliding step
Teiji-dachi	(teh-ee-jee dah-chee)	T stance
Tsugi ashi	(tsue-gee ash-ee)	Shuffling step
Tsumasaki	(tsue-mah-sah-key)	Tips of toes
Tsuru-ashi-dachi also *Gankaku-dachi* or *Sagi-ashi-dachi* (q.v.)	(tsue-roo-ah-shee dah-chee)	Crane stance
Uchi-hachiji-dachi	(oo-chee ha-chee-gee dah-chee)	Inverted open-leg stance
Yori ashi	(yoh-rhee ash-ee)	Dragging step
Zenkutsu-dachi	(zen-koo-tsue dah-chee)	Forward stance

General Terms

Agura	(ah-goo-rah)	Informal sitting (legs crossed)
Ai-uchi	(ah-ee-oo-chee)	Simultaneous points by both opponents in a match
Aka	(ah-kah)	Red (tournaments)
Ashi waza	(ah-shee wah-zah)	Foot/leg techniques
Attate Iru	(ah-tah-tay ih-roo)	Contact (tournaments)
Bo	(boh)	Staff, used as a weapon
Budo	(boo-doh)	Martial Way

Bunkai	(bun-kah-ee)	Study of kata applications and techniques
Chakuchki	(chaw-kutch-key)	Replacing
Chudan	(chew-dahn)	Chest area
Chui	(chew-ee)	Warning (tournaments)
Dan	(dahn)	Black belt rank
Do	(doh)	Way/Path
Do	(doh)	torso (target)
Dojo	(doh-joh)	Training gym (literally: *Place of the Way,* or *of Enlightenment*)
Domo Arigato Gozai-imasu	(doh-moh ah-ree-gah-toe go-zye-ih-mah-soo)	Thank you very much (present tense)
Domo Arigato Gozai-mashita	(doh-moh ah-ree-gah-toe go-zye-ih-mah-she-tah)	Thank you very much (past tense)
Embusen	(ehm-boo-sehn)	Pattern of a kata
Fujubun	(foo-jew-buhn)	Not enough power (tournaments)
Fukushin Shugo	(foo-koo-shin shoe-goh)	Judges conference (tournaments)
Gai-wan	(gah-ee wahn)	Outer arm
Gasshuku	(gas-shoe-koo)	Special training camp
Gedan	(geh-dahn)	Lower area of the body
Geri	(geh-rhee)	Kick
Gi	(ghee)	Jacket, Training costume
Gohon-Kumite	(goh-hon koo-mih-tay)	Five step basic sparring
Gokurosama	(goh-kuh-roh-sam-mah)	Thank you for doing what was expected of you (with respect)
Gokurosan	(goh-kuh-roh-san)	Thank you for doing what was expected of you.
Gyaku-do	(gyakoo-doh)	reverse (left side) torso (target)
Hai	(hah-ee)	Yes
Haishu	(hah-ee--shoo)	Backhand

Haisoku	(hah-ee-soh-koo)	Instep
Hajime	(hah-zhim-ay)	Begin
Hanshi	(hahn-she)	Head person of an organization
Hansoku	(hahn-soh-koo)	Foul, a penalty in tournament
Hantei	(hahn-tay)	Decision (tournaments)
Hidari	(he-dah-rhee)	Left
Hiji	(he-jee)	Elbow
Hiji-tori	(he-jee toh-ree)	grasping the elbow
Hikiwake	(hee-kee-wah-keh)	Draw in a match
Hiza	(he-zah)	Knee
Hombu-Dojo	(hohm-boo doh-joh)	Central dojo of an organization
Ippon	(eep-pohn)	One point in a match
Ippon kumite	(eep-pohn koo-me-teh)	One point sparring
Ippon shobu also *Shobu Ippon*	(eep-pohn show-boo)	One point match
Iye	(ee-yeh)	No
Jikan	(jee-kahn)	Time (tournaments)
Jiyu ippon kumite	(jee-yoo ih-pon koo-me-teh)	One step sparring from free stance
Jiyu-kumite	(jee-you koo-me-teh)	Free style sparring
Jo	(joh)	4'-5' wooden staff
Jo-sokutei	(joh so-koo-teh-ee)	Raised sole, also "Double Entry"
Jodan	(joh-dahn)	Face area
Jogai	(joh-guy)	Out of bounds (tournaments)
Kachi	(kah-chee)	Winner (tournaments)
Kaette	(kah-eh-teh)	Change
Kaisho	(kah-ee-show)	Open hand
Kakato	(kah-kah-toh)	Heel
Kakuto	(kah-koo-toh)	Bent-wrist
Kamae	(kah-mah-eh)	Combative posture
Kamae-te	(kah-mah-eh-teh)	Assume stance
Kansetsuwaza	(kahn-set-zu-wah-zah)	joint locking technique
Karate	(kah-rah-teh)	Empty-hand fighting
Karate-Do	(kah-rah-teh-doh)	The way of Karate
Karateka	(kah-rah-teh-kah)	A practitioner of karate
kata	(kah-tah)	Forms

Keiko	(kay-ee-koh)	Training
Keiko	(kay-ee-koh)	Joined fingertips
Keito	(kay-ee-toh)	Chicken-head wrist
Kendo	(ken-doh)	Sword fighting
Ken sen	(ken-sen)	sword tip
Kentsui	(ken-tsue-ee)	Fist hammer
Ki	(key)	Mind, Spirit, Energy
Kiai	(key-ah-ee)	Focusing shout, literally "Meeting of the spirits"
Kihon	(key-hohn)	Basic techniques
Kihon ippon	(key-hone ih-pon)	Basic one point sparring
Kihon kumite	(key-hone koo-me-teh)	Basic sparring
Kime	(key-may)	Focus of power
Ki-O-Tsuke	(key-oh-tsue-keh)	Attention
Kohai	(koh-hah-ee)	A student junior to oneself
Koken	(koh-ken)	Wrist Joint
Kon-ban-wa	(kohn-bahn-wah)	Good evening (after-daylight)
Konnichi-wa	(kohn-ee-chee-wah)	Good day (daylight hours)
Kobushi	(koh-boo-shih)	fist (holding sword)
Ko-shi	(koh-she)	Ball of the foot
Koshin	(koh-shin)	Rearward
Kote	(koh-the)	wrist
Kumite	(koo-me-teh)	Sparring
Kyoshi	(key-oh-she)	Master instructor
Kyu	(kyoo)	White/Brown belt rank
Ma	(mah)	Distance between opponents
Ma-ai	(mah-ah-ee)	Distancing
Ma-ai ga toh	(mah-ah-ee gah-toh)	Improper distancing (tournaments)
Mae	(mah-eh)	Front
Mae ukemi	(mah-eh oo-kehm-ee)	Front fall/roll
Makiwara	(mah-key-wha-rha)	Punching board
Matte	(mat-tay)	Wait
Mawaru	(mah-wha-roo)	To turn around
Mawat-te	(mah-wha-tay)	"Turn around."
Men	(men)	(fore-)head
Migi	(me-ghee)	Right
Mo-ichido	(moh-ee-chee-doh)	Once again

Mokuso	(moh-keh-so)	Silent contemplation, meditation
Morote no kamae	(moe-row-the no kah-may)	Augmented hand combative posture
Mudansha	(moo-dan-shah)	Students without black belt rank
Nagewaza	(nah-geh-wah-zah)	Throwing techniques
Nai-wan	(nah-ee wahn)	Inner arm
Nidan	(nee-dahn)	Second level (black belt)
Nukete iru	(noo-keh-tayee-roo)	Out of target (tournaments)
Nuki	(noo-key)	avoidance
Osae	(oh-sigh)	press down
O-suwate	(oh-swah-teh)	Sit down
O-tate	(oh-tah-teh)	Stand up
Obi	(oh-bee)	Belt
Ohaiyo Gozaimasu	(oh-ha-yoh go-zah-ee-mah-soo)	Good morning
Onegai-shimasu	(oh-neh-gah-ee-she-mah-soo)	Please teach me (literally "I make a request.")
Osu	(oh-soo)	Dojo greeting
Oyasumi nasai	(oh-yah-soo-me nah-sigh)	Good night (upon departing)
Oyo	(oh-yoh)	Study of techiques in kata, like *Bunkai,* but including follow-ups
Rei	(ray)	Bow
Reigi also *Reishiki*	(ray-ghee)	Etiquette
Reishiki also *Reigi*	(ray-she-key)	Etiquette
Renshi	(rehn-she)	Polished instructor
Renzoku waza	(rehn-zoh-koo wah-zah)	Combination techniques
Sanbon kumite	(san-bohn koo-me-teh)	Three step sparring
Sanbon-zuki	(san-bohn zoo-key)	Three punch combination
Sandan kumite	(san-dahn koo-me-teh)	Three step, three level sparring
Seigan	(say-gahn)	central sword posture

Seiza	(say-zah)	Proper sitting position on one's knees
Seme	(she-meh)	dominance
Sempai	(sehm-pye)	A senior student
Sensei	(sehn-seh-ee)	Instructor
Shiai	(shee-ah-ee)	Match
Shidachi	(shee-dah-chee)	answering sword
Shihan	(shee-han)	Formal title, Master Instructor, or "Teacher of Teachers"
Shiho-wari	(she-hoh wah-rhee)	Breaking boards on four sides to test power
Shimpan	(sheem-pahn)	Referee in a match
Shiro	(she-roh)	White
Shizen dachi no kamae	(she-zen dah-chee no kah-may)	Natural combative posture
Shizen-tai	(she-zen tah-ee)	Natural position
Shomen	(show-men)	The front
Sore made	(soh-reh mah-deh)	End of match
Suki	(sue-key)	Opening
Suriage	(soo-ree ah-gay)	sliding up
Tachi	(tah-chee)	Stances
Tachi zen	(tah-chee zen)	Standing meditation
Taimin ga osoi	(tah-ee-mean gah oh-soh-ee)	Not proper timing (tournaments)
Tai sabaki	(tah-ee sah-bah-key)	Body shifting
Tameshi-wari	(tah-meh-she-wah-rhee)	Test of technique's power
Tanden	(tahn-den)	Body center of mass
Tandoku renshu	(tan-doh-koo ren-shoe)	Preparatory exercise
Tenshin	(ten-shin)	Moving, shifting
Te waza	(teh wah-sah)	Hand attacks
Tome	(toh-may)	Finish
Tonfa	(tohn-fah)	Farm tool developed into weapon by Okinawans
Toranai	(toh-rah-nye)	No point (tournaments)
Torite	(toh-ree-teh)	Escape methods
Tsumeai	(tsoo-meh-aye)	pressure
Uchidachi	(oo-chee-dah-chee)	attacking sword
Uchi deshi	(oo-chee deh-she)	A live-in student
Ukete iru	(oo-keh-tay ee-roo)	Blocked (tournaments)

Ushiro	(oo-she-row)	Back, rear
Wan	(wahn)	Arm
Waza	(wah-zah)	Techniques
Waza-ari	(wah-zah ah-ree)	Half-point in a match
Yame	(yah-may)	Stop
Yasume	(yah-soo-me)	At ease
Yoi	(yoy)	Ready
Yoko	(yoh-koh)	Side
Yowai	(yow-wah-ee)	Weak focus (tournaments)
Yudansha	(you-dahn-shah)	Black belt holder
Zanshin	(zahn-sheen)	Following through technique literally, remaining mind/heart
Zazen	(zah-zen)	Meditation
Zenshin	(zehn-sheen)	Forward

Numbers

Ichi	(ih-chee)	One
Ni	(nee)	Two
San	(sahn)	Three
Shi	(she)	Four
Go	(go)	Five
Roku	(roh-koo)	Six
Shichi	(shih-chee)	Seven
Hachi	(hah-chee)	Eight
Ku	(koo)	Nine
Ju	(joo)	Ten

Appendix D
Class Outlines

On the following pages is a set of three class outlines appropriate to a *kihon*-centered beginners class, an intermediate or general ranks class, and a sparring class.

This schedule is designed to fit into a standard university three and one-half month semester schedule (specifically the University of Kentucky fall 1993 schedule), and finishes with the students prepared for a *kyu* rank test at the end of the semester (three per academic year).

In this training schedule, both the beginning and general classes meet for one hour each, two times per week (Monday and Wednesday), and the advanced (above green belt) class meets for an additional hour three times per week (Monday, Wednesday and Friday).

The schedule covers Monday and Wednesday evenings from 7:30 through 10:30 and Friday evenings from 7:30 to 8:30 (for the third sparring class). A further hour (Friday evenings from 8:30 to 9:30) is reserved for invitation only training, and generally involves brown and black belt *kata* study and practice.

This schedule provides the approximately 30 hours needed for the white and yellow belt ranks, and up to 60 hours for the green and brown belt ranks each semester. The invitational class can add another 15 hours of training for the upper rank students.

The schedule allows sufficient recovery on the days in between to prevent mental and physical deterioration, which can result from overtraining.

The university schedule also allows vacations from training between semesters. If the instructor is starting out with a new club, the same schedule will reserve time for personal training until the new students are sufficiently advanced to join the higher level class times. Such personal training, even if it is only repeated *kata* review, is critical so that the instructor does not lose too much skill while waiting for the development of the club, a matter of some two to three years. Having this self training out in view of the new students also gives them an idea of what they are aiming for in their practice, which builds enthusiasm.

This implies an "open" *dojo* atmosphere—anyone can come and see what is done at any time, no matter what their style or rank. If such visitors are legitimate martial artists, the new instructor has nothing to fear and everything to gain; if not, they will not stay around for long.

Additionally, I believe that some training always is better than no training—even spotty attendance by some students can be acceptable. Students will learn at their own pace and by their own motivation; this kind of learning cannot be forced. In time and with patience, attendance will improve, or the student will leave; in either case, there is no problem. Applying psychological harassment will only drive away those who can benefit most from the training.

In structuring the individual class time, I generally run formal warmup exercises only for the first month or so of the new semester; thereafter, the students are expected to arrive sufficiently early that they are warmed up and stretched out at the class starting time. Auxiliary strengthening exercises are also left to the student. I prefer to spend as much time on actual karate training as possible following the theory that practice produces improvement only in what is practiced, i.e., pushups are not punches. Strength and flexibility can be improved with karate practice with the concomitant advantage of learning technique, but strengthening and stretching exercises do not necessarily teach karate.

Finally, I believe that new instructors should teach only what they know and not be afraid of saying, "I don't know." This honesty will pay off in the long run; dishonesty or prevarication can lead only to eventual ruin.

D.1 Beginner

Class	Day	Date	Major Topic
1	wed	25-Aug	counterpunch, front stance
2	mon	30-Aug	up block, front kick
3	wed	01-Sep	outside & down block
4	mon	06-Sep	<labor day - no class>
5	wed	08-Sep	basic stepping
6	mon	13-Sep	3 step sparring
7	wed	15-Sep	back stance/knife hand
8	mon	20-Sep	*heian shodan*
9	wed	22-Sep	re-learn *kata*
10	mon	27-Sep	side snap kick
11	wed	29-Sep	side thrust kick
12	mon	04-Oct	basics review
13	wed	06-Oct	stepping review
14	mon	11-Oct	3 step sparring
15	wed	13-Oct	inside block, round kick
16	mon	18-Oct	correct *kata*
17	wed	20-Oct	resistance kicking
18	mon	25-Oct	work on *kata*
19	wed	27-Oct	belt kicking
20	mon	01-Nov	3-step sparring
21	wed	03-Nov	combinations
22	mon	08-Nov	*kata* training
23	wed	10-Nov	impact training
24	mon	15-Nov	pendulum practice
25	wed	17-Nov	test basics
26	mon	22-Nov	test practice
27	wed	24-Nov	individual practice
28	mon	29-Nov	standing review
29	wed	01-Dec	stepping review
30	mon	06-Dec	test practice
31	wed	08-Dec	*kyu* test (beginner)

D.2 Intermediate

Class	Day	Date	Major Topic
1	mon	23-Aug	<open>
2	wed	25-Aug	soft review
3	mon	30-Aug	stance training
4	wed	01-Sep	rotation techniques
5	mon	06-Sep	<Labor Day - none>
6	wed	08-Sep	learn new *kata*
7	mon	13-Sep	re-learn new *kata*
8	wed	15-Sep	pendulum training
9	mon	20-Sep	rotation shifting
10	wed	22-Sep	10-, 3-, & 1-step sparring
11	mon	27-Sep	combinations
12	wed	29-Sep	combinations
13	mon	04-Oct	1-step/side shifting
14	wed	06-Oct	1-step/circle shifting
15	mon	11-Oct	3- & 1-step sparring
16	wed	13-Oct	turning and spinning
17	mon	18-Oct	step through *kata*
18	wed	20-Oct	resistance kicking
19	mon	25-Oct	work on *kata*
20	wed	27-Oct	belt kicking
21	mon	01-Nov	3- & 1-step sparring
22	wed	03-Nov	more combinations
23	mon	08-Nov	*kata* training
24	wed	10-Nov	impact training
25	mon	15-Nov	3-step pendulum
26	wed	17-Nov	test basics
27	mon	22-Nov	test practice
28	wed	24-Nov	individual *kata*
29	mon	29-Nov	standing review
30	wed	01-Dec	stepping review
31	mon	06-Dec	test practice
32	wed	08-Dec	*kyu* test (intermediates)

D.3 Advanced

Note: Friday classes were in a room with mats and therefore had occasional classes on throwing and falling.

Class	Day	Date	Major Topic
1	mon	23-Aug	<open>
2	wed	25-Aug	slide punches
3	fri	27-Aug	slide lunges
4	mon	30-Aug	slide step combinations
5	wed	01-Sep	stance snap shifting
6	fri	03-Sep	spot pushing kicks
7	mon	06-Sep	<Labor Day - none>
8	wed	08-Sep	learn new *kata*
9	fri	10-Sep	*kata bunkai*
10	mon	13-Sep	attack combinations
11	wed	15-Sep	attack combinations
12	fri	17-Sep	sweep attacks
13	mon	20-Sep	corner entries
14	wed	22-Sep	semi-free 1-step
15	fri	24-Sep	slaughterline
16	mon	27-Sep	parrying practice
17	wed	29-Sep	semi-free 1-step
18	fri	01-Oct	semi-free 1-step
19	mon	04-Oct	semi-free 1-step
20	wed	06-Oct	semi-free 1-step
21	fri	08-Oct	hook kicking
22	mon	11-Oct	extended response pendulum
23	wed	13-Oct	extended response pendulum
24	fri	15-Oct	throws
25	mon	18-Oct	directed free
26	wed	20-Oct	directed free
27	fri	22-Oct	throws
28	mon	25-Oct	work on *kata*
29	wed	27-Oct	positioning training
30	fri	29-Oct	positioning training
31	mon	01-Nov	positioning training
32	wed	03-Nov	2-step positioning
33	fri	05-Nov	throw rollouts

D.3 Advanced (continued)

Class	Day	Date	Major Topic
34	mon	08-Nov	2-step positioning
35	wed	10-Nov	impact training
36	fri	12-Nov	*kata bunkai*
37	mon	15-Nov	directed free
38	wed	17-Nov	2-minute rounds
39	fri	19-Nov	push rollouts
40	mon	22-Nov	round robin
41	wed	24-Nov	individual *kata*
42	fri	26-Nov	<Thanksgiving - none>
43	mon	29-Nov	test techniques
44	wed	01-Dec	individual *kata*
45	fri	03-Dec	advanced *bunkai*
46	mon	08-Dec	test practice
47	wed	10-Dec	*kyu* test (advanced)

Appendix E
Rank Test Requirements

There are several philosophies prevalent in designing ranking examinations.

Examinations can be designed as a true test of passage, stressing the student to the limits of physical and mental endurance. This can involve pushups, multiple *kumite*, and days of testing.

Alternatively, they can be made as intellectually challenging as possible, using techniques and combinations never practiced before, thus stressing the student's ability to apply what has been learned to novel situations. In this form, the instructor develops a set of combinations for the test designed to reveal weaknesses in the student's balance and body dynamics. In my opinion, this format has the danger that the students are psychologically in opposition to the instructor.

Some schools also include a written component for the rank tests.

My personal preference is a third way: To make the rank exam itself relatively simple and explicit, so that there are no surprises for the student. I also prefer to keep the test physical, avoiding written requirements, trusting instead that understanding can be demonstrated best with performance rather than with words.

The advantage of this format is that it provides the students with the chance to show their best, with only their own ability determining their success or failure. The criteria for passing any particular rank also remain fixed and well known.

What the instructor must keep clear is what each rank is *not* required to know. It is easy to let an inflation of the grading severity creep in so that each time the tests become just a little bit harder to pass. The criteria of how much power, how much speed, and the level of accuracy and precision must remain stable, or the students will lose faith in their ability to improve and fall victim to the perception that each is getting worse rather than better with training.

My philosophy is colored by my upbringing in karate. There were 4 qualitative ranks (white, green, brown and black), and within each were quantitative ranks (the kyu levels within each color, with 6th kyu, 3rd kyu and shodan being the first ranks of the new colors). So the quantitative ranks were easily defined as "more and better of the same," and rarely had a failure rate exceeding 10%. The qualitative ranks were the ranks that generally had a significant failure rate (around 20% at green, around 60% at brown and around 90% at first try at black).

I think that this way of looking at the kyu rankings simplifies things and matches onto many shotokan students' experience of how people clump up in their learning. So for me at least, white belts are expected to "not fall over" either mentally or physically while performing the required techniques. Green belts are expected to do the techniques correctly, with proper sequencing of body components in space and time. Brown belts are expected to show power in addition. And black belts are expected to show that the techniques are (so to speak) "doing" them, rather than they doing techniques, i.e., completely internalized (see Chapter 12: Styles and Methods).

As an example, the charts that follow provide a set of test techniques to be demonstrated when testing for the rank indicated. In general, the charts follow the requirements of the Japan Karate Association.

In this test format, students are examined in pairs. *Kata* is performed first, followed by the demonstration of basics. The test techniques listed are performed upon command by count, each technique listed performed between six and eight times, and each basic series is performed in one direction, either stepping forward or backward in turn. Then the pair of students face each other for the sparring section of the test.

RANK:	8-*KYU*	7-*KYU*	6-*KYU*
	[YELLOW BELT]	[YELLOW BELT]	[GREEN BELT]
KATA: (FORMS)	Heian Shodan	Heian Nidan	Heian Sandan
KUMITE: (SPARRING)	3-step (counted) face stomach	3-step (counted) face stomach	1-step face stomach front kick

KIHON: (BASICS)	step punch (mid)
	rising block
	outside block
	knife hand block
	front kick (mid)
	front kick (head)
	side snap kick
	side thrust kick
	front kick +
	    stepping punch
		step punch (head)
		rising block
		outside block
		inside block
		backfist (head)
		knife hand block
		front kick (h)
		round kick (m)
		side snap kick
		side thrust kick
		front kick +
		    stepping punch
		round kick +
		    counterpunch
			triple punch
			rising block+
			    counterpunch
			outside block+
			    counterpunch (h)
			inside block+
			    counterpunch (h)
			backfist+
			    counterpunch
			knife hand block+
			    spear hand
			front kick (mid)+
			    front kick (head)
			round kick (head)
			side snap kick
			side thrust kick
			front kick +
			    stepping punch
			round kick +
			    counterpunch
			front kick +
			    round kick

RANK:	5-*KYU*	4-*KYU*	3-*KYU*
	[GREEN BELT]	[GREEN BELT]	[BROWN BELT]
KATA:	Heian Yondan	Heian Godan	Tekki Shodan
KUMITE:	1-step face stomach front kick roundhouse kick	1-step face stomach front kick roundhouse kick side thrust kick	1-step (semi-free) face stomach front kick roundhouse kick side thrust kick spin back kick

(Continued)	5-KYU	4-KYU	3-KYU
	[GREEN BELT]	[GREEN BELT]	[BROWN BELT]
KIHON:	triple punch rising block+ 　counterpunch outside block+ 　elbow attack inside block+ 　counterpunch backfist+ 　counterpunch knife hand block+ 　fr leg fr kick + 　spear hand front kick (mid)+ 　front kick (head) round kick (mid)+ 　round kick (head) side snap kick 　side thrust kick front kick + 　stepping punch round kick + 　counterpunch front kick + 　round kick + 　counterpunch	triple punch rising block+ 　counterpunch outside block+ 　elbow attack+ 　counterpunch inside block+ 　counterpunch backfist+ 　counterpunch knife hand block+ 　fr leg fr kick + 　spear hand front kick (mid)+ 　front kick (head) round kick (mid)+ 　round kick (head) side snap kick side thrust kick front kick + 　stepping punch round kick + 　counterpunch front kick + 　round kick + 　side thrust	triple punch rising block+ 　fr leg fr kick+ 　counterpunch outside block+ 　elbow attack+ 　backfist+ 　counterpunch inside block+ 　lead hand punch+ 　counterpunch step punch + 　backfist+ 　counterpunch knife hand block+ 　fr leg fr kick + 　spear hand fr leg fr kick+ 　front kick(m+h) fr leg rnd kick+ 　round kick (m+h) side snap kick side thrust kick front kick + 　round kick + 　side thrust+ 　spin back kick fr + s snap kick fr + s thr kick pencil punch

RANK:	2-KYU	1-KYU
	[BROWN BELT]	[BROWN BELT]
KATA:	*Tekki Nidan,* *Jion, Kanku Dai,* or *Bassai Dai* & <choice>	*Tekki Sandan,* *Jion, Kanku Dai,* or *Bassai Dai* & <choice>
KUMITE:	[same as 3-*kyu*] + directed free	[same as 2-*kyu*]
KIHON:	[same as 3-*kyu*]	[same as 3-*kyu*]

RANK: **1st DAN**

[BLACK BELT]

KATA:	1	Jion, Kanku Dai, Bassai Dai, Tekki Nidan or Sandan	KIHON:	1	triple punch
	2	& <assigned>		2	rising block+ fr leg fr kick+ ounterpunch
KUMITE:		1-step (semi-free)		3	outside block+ elbow attack+ backfist+ counterpunch
	1	face			
	2	stomach			
	3	front kick		4	inside block+ lead hand punch+ counterpunch
	4	roundhouse kick			
	5	side thrust kick			
	6	spin back kick		5	step punch + backfist+ counterpunch
		+ directed free			
				6	knife hand block+ fr leg fr kick + spear hand
				7	fr leg fr kick+ front kick(m+h)
				8	fr leg rnd kick+ round kick (m+h)
				9	side snap kick w/ side thrust kick
				10	front kick + round kick + side thrust+ spin back kick
				11	bk leg rnd kick w/ side thrust + counterpunch
				12	fr leg rnd kick w/ side thrust + step punch
				13	3x step punch
				14	outside block, lead hand punch w/ fr leg fr kick, counterpunch
				15	fr + s snap + thr kick
				16	pencil punch

Advanced *Dan* Ranks:

(Examiner & examinee each pick one *kata* from list, not including *Heian* or *Tekki kata*)

2nd *Dan* Kata
(all previous +)
Bassai Sho
Enpi
Gankaku
Hangetsu
Jitte
Kanku Sho
Sochin

2nd *Dan* Kumite

5 techniques against:
a: stepping punch
b: front kick

directed free:
(attack/defense)

2nd *Dan* Kihon (4 sets each)

1	Lead hand punch + stepping triple punch
(turn) 2	Lead hand punch + front kick w/ stepping punch
(turn) 3	step back w/ up block + step in round kick + backfist + step in punch
4	stepping back w/ front, round, side thrust, spin, & back kicks & counterpunch
5	(side shift) side snap w/ side thrust kick
6	(in place) front + side snap + side thrust + round + back kick (each leg)

3rd *Dan* Kata
(all previous +)
Chinte
Gojushiho Dai
Gojushiho Sho
Ji'in
Meikyo
Nijushiho
Unsu
Wankan

3rd *Dan* Kumite
free sparring vs
a: below 2nd *Dan*
b: at 2nd *Dan*
c: above 2nd *Dan*

3rd *Dan* Kihon

1 - 6	(Same as 2nd Dan, but from memory)

3rd *Dan* Additional

1	self defense against grab w/ punch (3 attacks)
2	self defense against club (3 attacks)
3	self defense against knife (3 attacks)

Appendix F
Kata:
In-Breath Forms

The *kata* are presented here in a skeletonized form, listing the instructor's counts for single technique, short sequence (SS) and long sequence (LS) practice, as well as the approximate direction of the main technique and its breath (in or out) with a few accompanying comments to clarify some of the linkages.

I have separated the short sequences from each other with single lines, and the long sequences with double lines.

Also, I have tried to make the short sequences apply to one opponent at a time, i.e., they are set up as self-defense combinations.

Each *kata's* long sequences are designed more for a mixed class group practice, so they are somewhat arbitrarily set at three per *kata*. How the instructor decides to split up the counts for each *kata*, and which *kata* are compatible with each other in the same training period are personal decisions based on the instructor's feeling for the combinations and applications.

With group practice using counts, some pauses will always feel forced for some *kata*. It is presumed that the reader already knows the physical movements, sequence, and speed of each technique in these *kata*; they cannot be learned from these lists.

Directions are stated with the starting position pointing to the north, or the front (for the *Tekki kata*). Subsequent directions are given either by compass headings or left/right, as appropriate.

The basic *kata* (*Heian* and *Tekki*) are given first, then the intermediate and advanced forms in alphabetical order.

Gojushiho Dai and *Sho* are indicated with their alternate names (*Useshi* and *Hotaku*) because there are differences between the various organizations as to which is to be called *sho* and which *dai*.

These breathing and linkage directions are not absolute; alternatives do exist and are useful in their own ways.

F.1 Heian Shodan

STEP	SS	LS	TECHNIQUE	DIR	BREATH	NOTES
1	0	0	READY	N	OUT	BEGIN
2	1	1	DOWN BLOCK	W	IN	LINK
3	1	1	STEP PUNCH	W	OUT	PAUSE
4	2	1	DOWN BLOCK	E	IN	180 CW
5	2	1	HAMMER FIST	E	OUT	SWING, LINK
6	2	1	STEP PUNCH	E	OUT	STEP BREATH
7	3	1	DOWN BLOCK	N	IN	90 CCW, PAUSE
8	3	1	STEP UP BLOCK	N	OUT	PAUSE
9	3	1	STEP UP BLOCK	N	IN	LINK
10	3	1	STEP UP BLOCK	N	OUT	KIAI, WAIT
11	4	2	DOWN BLOCK	E	IN	270 CCW
12	4	2	STEP PUNCH	E	OUT	PAUSE
13	5	2	DOWN BLOCK	W	IN	180 CW
14	5	2	STEP PUNCH	W	OUT	PAUSE
15	6	2	DOWN BLOCK	S	IN	PAUSE
16	6	2	STEP PUNCH	S	OUT	PAUSE
17	6	2	STEP PUNCH	S	IN	LINK
18	6	2	STEP PUNCH	S	OUT	KIAI, WAIT
19	7	3	KNIFE HAND	E	IN	LINK
20	7	3	KNIFE HAND	NE	OUT	PAUSE
21	8	3	KNIFE HAND	W	IN	LINK
22	8	3	KNIFE HAND	NW	OUT	PAUSE
23	0	0	ENDING	N	IN,OUT	STOP

F.2 Heian Nidan

STEP	SS	LS	TECHNIQUE	DIR	BREATH	NOTES
1	0	0	READY	N	OUT	BEGIN
2	1	1	UP/HAMMER	W	IN	90 CCW
3	1	1	CROSS/HAMMER	W	OUT	STEP LINK
4	1	1	PULL/HAMMER	W	OUT	PAUSE
5	2	1	UP/HAMMER	E	IN	180 CW
6	2	1	CROSS/HAMMER	E	OUT	STEP LINK
7	2	1	PULL/HAMMER	E	OUT	PAUSE
8	3	1	SIDE SNAP/ BACKFIST	S	IN	90 CW
9	3	1	KNIFE HAND	N	OUT	180 CCW
10	4	1	KNIFE HAND	N	IN,OUT	PAUSE
11	4	1	KNIFE HAND	N	IN	LINK
12	4	1	SPEAR HAND	N	OUT	KIAI, WAIT
13	5	2	KNIFE HAND	E	IN	LINK
14	5	2	KNIFE HAND	SE	OUT	PAUSE
15	6	2	KNIFE HAND	W	IN	LINK
16	6	2	KNIFE HAND	SW	OUT	PAUSE
17	7	2	COUNTER IN BLOCK	S	IN,OUT	REVERSE HIP
18	7	2	FRONT KICK	S	IN	FLOW THROUGH
19	7	2	COUNTERPUNCH	S	OUT	STEP BREATH
20	7	2	COUNTER IN BLOCK	S	OUT	LINK
21	7	2	FRONT KICK	S	IN	FLOW THROUGH
22	7	2	COUNTERPUNCH	S	OUT	STEP BREATH
23	7	2	AUGMENTED BLOCK	S	OUT	PAUSE
24	8	3	DOWN BLOCK	E	IN	270 CCW
25	8	3	PALM PARR	NE	OUT	45 CW, STEP BREATH
26	8	3	UP BLOCK	NE	OUT	PAUSE
27	9	3	DOWN BLOCK	W	IN	135 CW
28	9	3	PALM PARRY	NW	OUT	STEP BREATH
29	9	3	UP BLOCK	NW	OUT	KIAI
30	0	0	RETURN	N	IN,OUT	STOP

F.3 Heian Sandan

STEP	SS	LS	TECHNIQUE	DIR	BREATH	NOTES
1	0	0	READY	N	OUT	BEGIN
2	1	1	INSIDE BLOCK	W	IN	90 CCW
3	1	1	DOUBLE FISTS	W	OUT	STEP BREATH
4	1	1	DOUBLE FISTS	W	OUT	
5	2	1	INSIDE BLOCK	E	IN	180 CCW
6	2	1	DOUBLE FISTS	E	OUT	STEP BREATHS
7	2	1	DOUBLE FISTS	E	OUT	
8	3	1	AUGM. BLOCK	N	IN	90 CW
9	3	1	PARRY, SPEAR HAND	N	OUT	
10	3	1	HAMMER FIST	N	IN	270 CCW SPIN
11	3	1	STEPPING PUNCH	N	OUT	KIAI, WAIT
12	4	2	STANDING TURN	S	IN,OUT	180 CCW, SLOW
13	5	2	SHIN BLOCK	S	IN	
14	5	2	STOMP W/ BLOCK	S	OUT	STEP BREATH
15	5	2	BACKFIST	S	OUT	
16	5	2	SHIN BLOCK	S	IN	
17	5	2	STOMP W/ BLOCK	S	OUT	STEP BREATH
18	5	2	BACKFIST	S	OUT	
19	5	2	SHIN BLOCK	S	IN	
20	5	2	STOMP W/ BLOCK	S	OUT	STEP BREATH
21	5	2	BACKFIST	S	OUT	
22	6	3	STANDING KNIFE	S	IN	SLOW
23	6	3	STEPPING PUNCH	S	OUT	
24	7	3	STEP UP	S	IN	ADJUST FEET
25	7	3	DIRECT THROW	N	OUT	SPIN, STEP BREATH
26	7	3	REVERSE THROW	N	OUT	KIAI, WAIT
27	0	0	ENDING	N	IN,OUT	

F.4 Heian Yondan

STEP	SS	LS	TECHNIQUE	DIR	BREATH	NOTES
1	0	0	READY	N	OUT	BEGIN
2	1	1	DOUBLE KNIFE HAND	W	IN	90 CCW
3	1	1	DOUBLE KNIFE HAND	E	OUT	180 CW
4	1	1	LOW "X" BLOCK	N	IN	90 CCW
5	1	1	AUGMENTED BLOCK	N	OUT	PAUSE
6	2	1	SIDE SNAP/BACKFIST	W	IN	90 CCW
7	2	1	REACH, ELBOW SMASH	W	OUT	
8	2	1	SIDE SNAP/BACKFIST	E	IN	ADJUST FEET, 180 CW
9	2	1	REACH, ELBOW SMASH	E	OUT	
10	3	1	DOWN & UP BLOCKS	N	IN	REVERSE HIP
11	3	1	CHOP W/ UP BLOCK	N	OUT	90 CCW
12	3	1	FRONT KICK	N	IN	LINK
13	3	1	GRAB & BACKFIST	N	OUT	KIAI, WAIT
14	4	2	WEDGE BLOCK	SE	IN,OUT	225 CCW, SLOW
15	4	2	FRONT KICK	SE	IN	LINK
16	4	2	DOUBLE PUNCH	SE	OUT,OUT	VIBRATION
17	5	2	WEDGE BLOCK	SW	IN,OUT	90 CW, SLOW
18	5	2	FRONT KICK	SW	IN	LINK
19	5	2	DOUBLE PUNCH	SW	OUT,OUT	VIBRATION
20	6	3	AUGMENTED BLOCK	S	IN	45 CCW
21	6	3	AUGMENTED BLOCK	S	OUT	
22	7	3	AUGMENTED BLOCK	S	IN	LINK
23	7	3	HEAD GRAB	S	IN	
24	7	3	KNEE SMASH	S	OUT	KIAI, LINK
25	7	3	KNIFE HAND	N	IN	
26	7	3	KNIFE HAND	N	OUT	
27	0	0	ENDING	N	IN,OUT	STOP

F.5 Heian Godan

STEP	SS	LS	TECHNIQUE	DIR	BREATH	NOTES
1	0	0	READY	N	OUT	BEGIN
2	1	1	INSIDE BLOCK	E	IN	90 CCW, LINK
3	1	1	COUNTER PUNCH	E	OUT	PAUSE
4	1	1	HOOK PUNCH	N	IN,OUT	90 CW, STAND, SLOW
5	2	1	INSIDE BLOCK	W	IN	90 CW, LINK
6	2	1	COUNTER PUNCH	W	OUT	PAUSE
7	2	1	HOOK PUNCH	N	IN,OUT	90 CCW, STAND SLOW
8	3	1	AUGMENTED BLOCK	N	IN	LINK
9	3	1	LOW X-BLOCK	N	OUT	
10	3	1	UP X-BLOCK	N	IN	LINK
11	3	1	WRIST TWIST/PULL	N	OUT	
12	3	1	HAMMER FIST	N	IN	LINK, QUICK
13	3	1	STEPPING PUNCH	N	OUT	KIAI, WAIT
14	4	2	SPIN STOMP/DOWN BLOCK	S	IN,OUT	180 CCW
15	4	2	BACK HAND	N	IN	SLOW
16	4	2	CRESCENT KICK/ ELBOW	E	OUT,OUT	180 CCW
17	5	2	AUGMENTED BLOCK	N	IN	90 CW, TWIST STANCE
18	5	2	STANDING THRUST	N	OUT	TURN AWAY
19	5	2	JUMPING LOW X-BLOCK	W	IN,OUT	180 CCW, KIAI
20	5	2	AUGMENTED BLOCK	S	OUT	90 CW, PAUSE
21	6	3	REACH	N	IN	180 CCW
22	6	3	PARRY W/ LOW THRUST	N	OUT	LINK, STEP BREATH
23	6	3	LOW & HIGH THROW	N	OUT	PAUSE
24	6	3	STAND UP	N	IN,OUT	SLOW
25	7	3	SPIN & REACH	N	IN	180 CCW
26	7	3	PARRY W/ LOW THRUST	N	OUT	LINK, STEP BREATH
27	7	3	LOW & HIGH (THROW)	N	OUT	PAUSE
28	0	0	ENDING	N	IN,OUT	STOP

F.6 Tekki Shodan

STEP	SS	LS	TECHNIQUE	DIR	BREATH	NOTES
1	0	0	READY	FR	OUT	BEGIN
2	1	1	DROP	RI	IN	LINK
3	1	1	BACK HAND	RI	OUT	
4	1	1	ELBOW STRIKE	RI	IN	
5	1	1	HAND SET (THROW)	LE	OUT	
6	1	1	DOWN BLOCK	LE	IN	
7	1	1	HOOK PUNCH	LE	OUT	
8	2	1	STEP ACROSS	LE	IN	SLOW
9	2	1	INSIDE BLOCK	FR	OUT	
10	2	1	DOUBLE BLOCK	FR	IN	QUICK LINK
11	2	1	INVERTED THRUST	FR	OUT	
12	3	1	WAVE KICK	LE	IN	LINK
13	3	1	AUGMENTED BLOCK	LE	OUT	
14	3	1	WAVE KICK	RI	IN	LINK
15	3	1	AUGMENTED BLOCK	RI	OUT	
16	4	1	HAND SET (THROW)	LE	IN	QUICK LINK
17	4	1	DOUBLE THRUST	LE	OUT	KIAI, WAIT
18	5	2	BACK HAND	LE	IN,OUT	SLOW
19	6	3	ELBOW STRIKE	LE	IN	
20	6	3	HAND SET (THROW)	RI	OUT	
21	6	3	DOWN BLOCK	RI	IN	
22	6	3	HOOK PUNCH	RI	OUT	
23	7	3	STEP ACROSS	RI	IN	SLOW
24	7	3	INSIDE BLOCK	FR	OUT	
25	7	3	DOUBLE BLOCK	FR	IN	QUICK LINK
26	7	3	INVERTED THRUST	FR	OUT	
27	8	3	WAVE KICK	RI	IN	LINK
28	8	3	AUGMENTED BLOCK	RI	OUT	
29	8	3	WAVE KICK	LE	IN	LINK
30	8	3	AUGMENTED BLOCK	LE	OUT	
31	9	3	HAND SET (THROW)	RI	IN	QUICK LINK
32	9	3	DOUBLE THRUST	RI	OUT	KIAI, WAIT
33	0	0	RETURN	FR	IN,OUT	SLOW
34	0	0	ENDING	FR	IN,OUT	STOP

F.7 Tekki Nidan

STEP	SS	LS	TECHNIQUE	DIR	BREATH	NOTES
1	0	0	READY	FR	OUT	BEGIN
2	1	1	RISING ELBOWS	RT	IN	SLOW
3	1	1	STOMP W/ WEDGE BLOCK	RT	OUT	
4	1	1	SWEEP GROIN	RT	IN	LINK
5	1	1	PUSH ARM	RT	OUT	PAUSE
6	2	1	STAND W/ RISING ELBOWS	LF	IN	SLOW
7	2	1	STOMP W/ WEDGE BLOCK	LF	OUT	
8	2	1	SWEEP GROIN	LF	IN	LINK
9	2	1	PUSH ARM	LF	OUT	PAUSE
10	3	2	PULL & SET HAND	FR	IN	LINK
11	3	2	INSIDE BLOCK	FR	OUT	
12	3	2	PULL & SET HAND W/ KNEE	FR	IN	LINK
13	3	2	ELBOW STRIKE W/ STOMP	FR	OUT	
14	3	2	OPENING KNIFE HAND	RT	IN	SLOW
15	3	2	HOOK PUNCH	RT	OUT	
16	4	2	BIG STEP ACROSS	RT	IN	SLOW
17	4	2	INSIDE BLOCK W/STOMP	RT	OUT	
18	4	2	DOUBLE BLOCK	FR	IN	LINK
19	4	2	INVERTED THRUST	FR	OUT	KIAI
20	5	3	PULL & SET HAND	FR	IN	LINK
21	5	3	INSIDE BLOCK	FR	OUT	
22	5	3	PULL & SET HAND W/ KNEE	FR	IN	LINK
23	5	3	ELBOW STRIKE W/ STOMP	FR	OUT	
24	5	3	OPENING KNIFE HAND	LE	IN	SLOW
25	5	3	HOOK PUNCH	LE	OUT	
26	6	3	BIG STEP ACROSS	LE	IN	SLOW
27	6	3	INSIDE BLOCK W/ STOMP	FR	OUT	
28	6	3	DOUBLE BLOCK	FR	IN	LINK
29	6	3	INVERTED THRUST	FR	OUT	KIAI
30	0	0	ENDING	FR	IN,OUT	STOP

F.8 Tekki Sandan

STEP	SS	LS	TECHNIQUE	DIR	BREATH	NOTES
1	0	0	READY	FR	OUT	BEGIN
2	1	1	INSIDE BLOCK	FR	IN	
3	1	1	DOUBLE BLOCK	FR	OUT	PAUSE
4	1	1	CROSS PALMHEELS	FR	IN	LINK
5	1	1	PULLING BLOCK	FR	IN	LINK
6	1	1	INVERTED THRUST (SNAP)	FR	OUT	LINK
7	1	1	FRONT THRUST	FR	OUT	
8	1	1	TURN HAND	RT	IN,OUT	SLOW
9	2	1	LOW STEP ACROSS	RT	IN	SLOW
10	2	1	SWEEP BLOCK	RT	OUT	
11	2	1	CIRCLE THROW	RT	IN,OUT	
12	3	1	PULL HAND	FR	IN	
13	3	1	PUNCH	FR	OUT	LINK
14	3	1	DOUBLE BLOCK	FR	OUT	
15	3	1	DOUBLE BLOCK	FR	IN	LINK
16	3	1	PULLING UPBLOCK	FR	IN	LINK
17	3	1	INVERTED THRUST	FR	OUT	KIAI, WAIT
18	4	2	BIG STEP ACROSS	LE	IN	SLOW
19	4	2	STOMP W/INSIDE BLOCK	FR	OUT	PAUSE
20	4	2	CROSS PALMHEELS	FR	IN	LINK
21	4	2	PULLING BLOCK	FR	IN	LINK
22	4	2	INVERTED THRUST (SNAP)	FR	OUT	LINK
23	4	2	FRONT THRUST	FR	OUT	
24	4	2	TURN HAND	LE	IN,OUT	SLOW
25	5	2	LOW STEP ACROSS	LE	IN	SLOW
26	5	2	SWEEP BLOCK	LE	OUT	
27	5	2	CIRCLE THROW	LE	IN,OUT	
28	6	3	PULL HAND	LE	IN	
29	6	3	PUNCH	FR	OUT	
30	6	3	OPENING KNIFE HAND	RT	IN	SLOW
31	6	3	HOOK PUNCH	RT	OUT	
32	7	3	BIG STEP ACROSS	RT	IN	SLOW
33	7	3	STOMP W/INSIDE BLOCK	FR	OUT	
34	7	3	DOUBLE BLOCK	FR	IN	LINK
35	7	3	PULLING UPBLOCK	FR	IN	LINK
36	7	3	INVERTED THRUST	FR	OUT	KIAI, WAIT
37	0	0	ENDING	FR	IN,OUT	STOP

F.9 Bassai Dai

STEP	SS	LS	TECHNIQUE	DIR	BREATH	NOTES
1	0	0	YOI	N	OUT	READY
2	1	1	PULL HANDS; BACKFIST	N	IN,OUT	LINK, QUICK
3	1	1	SPIN, INSIDE BLOCK	S	IN	
4	1	1	COUNTER OUTSIDE BLOCK	S	OUT	
5	2	1	SPIN, CTR. OUT. BLOCK	N	IN	
6	2	1	INSIDE BLOCK	N	OUT	
7	3	1	SQUAT, SCOOP, LIFT	E	IN	
8	3	1	OUTSIDE BLOCK	E	OUT	LINK
9	3	1	COUNTER INSIDE BLOCK	E	OUT	
10	4	1	SET HANDS, STAND	N	IN,OUT	SLOW
11	4	1	STANDING KNIFE HAND	N	IN	SLOW
12	4	1	PUNCH, IN. BLOCK	N	OUT, OUT	LINK, STEP BREATH
13	4	1	WAIT; PUNCH, IN. BLOCK	N	IN;O, O	LINKED, STEP BREATH
14	5	1	SHIFT, KNIFE HAND	N	IN, IN	
15	5	1	KNIFE HAND	N	OUT	
16	5	1	KNIFE HAND	N	IN	LINK
17	5	1	RETREATING KNIFE HAND	N	OUT	
18	6	2	SWING HANDS	N	IN	
19	6	2	TRAP HANDS	N	OUT	
20	6	2	LIFT LEG	N	IN	
21	6	2	CUTTING KICK	N	OUT	KIAI
22	6	2	TURN, KNIFE HAND	S	IN	
23	6	2	KNIFE HAND	S	OUT	
24	7	2	PULL BACK, LIFT HANDS	S	IN	SLOW
25	7	2	DOUBLE HAMMER	S	OUT	LINK, STEP BREATH
26	7	2	SLIDE PUNCH	S	OUT	
27	8	2	TURN & REACH	N	IN	
28	8	2	PARRY, LOW PALM HEEL	N	OUT	
29	8	2	STAND, HIGH & LOW	E	IN	SLOW
30	8	2	TURN, STOMP, DN BLOCK	W	OUT	
31	9	2	BACK HAND BLOCK	E	IN	
32	9	2	CRESCENT KICK, ELBOW	W	OUT,OUT	STEP BREATH
33	9	2	DOWN HAMMER	W	IN	
34	9	2	2 MORE	W	OUT,OUT	STEP BREATH

continued on next page

F.9 Bassai Dai (continued)

STEP	SS	LS	TECHNIQUE	DIR	BREATH	NOTES
35	10	3	PULL HANDS, SHIFT	S	IN	SET STANCE
36	10	3	KNEE LIFT, C-PUNCH	S	OUT	
37	10	3	PULL BACK	S	IN	SLOW
38	10	3	KNEE LIFT, C-PUNCH	S	OUT	
39	10	3	PULL BACK	S	IN	SLOW
40	10	3	KNEE LIFT, C-PUNCH	S	OUT	
41	11	3	SPIN, SCOOP	N	IN	
42	11	3	REV. INSIDE BLOCK	N	OUT	
43	11	3	SCOOP	N	IN	
44	11	3	REV. INSIDE BLOCK	N	OUT	
45	12	3	STEP UP, KNIFE HAND	NE	IN,OUT	LINK
46	12	3	DRAWING KNIFE HAND	SE	IN	SLOW
47	12	3	STEP UP KNIFE HAND	NW	OUT	KIAI
48	0	0	YAME	N	IN,OUT	STOP

F.10 Bassai Sho

STEP	SS	LS	TECHNIQUE	DIR	BREATH	NOTES
1	0	0	YOI	N	OUT	READY
2	1	1	TWIST&PULL, SWING HANDS	N	IN, OUT	ENTER, TWIST STANCE
3	1	1	TURN, CATCH STAFF	S	IN	
4	1	1	LEVER UP	S	OUT	SLOW
5	2	1	SPIN, SCOOP BLOCK	E	IN	
6	2	1	SWING DOWN BLOCK	E	OUT	
7	2	1	STEP IN, CATCH STAFF	E	IN	
8	2	1	LEVER UP	E	OUT	SLOW
9	3	1	PULL BACK, SET UP	N	IN	
10	3	1	SIDE SNAP, RIDGE HAND	N	OUT	ATTACK TO E
11	3	1	STANDING KNIFE HAND	N	IN	
12	3	1	DOUBLE PUNCH	N	OUT, OUT	STEP BREATH
13	3	1	HIGH & LOW	W	IN	
14	3	1	HIGH & LOW	E	OUT	
15	4	2	SHIFT, KNIFE HAND	N	IN	
16	4	2	STEP KNIFE HAND	N	OUT	
17	4	2	STEP KNIFE HAND	N	IN	LINK
18	4	2	PULL BACK, KNIFE HAND	N	OUT	
19	5	2	SWING HANDS	N	IN	
20	5	2	WRIST BREAK	N	OUT	SLOW
21	5	2	CUTTING KICK	N	IN, OUT	KIAI
22	5	2	TURN, INSIDE WEDGE	S	IN	
23	5	2	SLIDE, DOUBLE THRUST	S	OUT	
24	5	2	PULL W/ ARMS & LEG	S	IN	
25	5	2	DOUBLE SIDE PUNCH	S	OUT	
26	6	2	HAMMER FIST	N	IN	
27	6	2	STEP PUNCH	N	OUT	KIAI
28	7	3	SPIN, PULL	S	IN	
29	7	3	DOUBLE SIDE PUNCH	S	OUT	
30	7	3	TURN, PULL	S	IN	
31	7	3	DOUBLE SIDE PUNCH	S	OUT	
32	7	3	TURN, PULL	S	IN	
33	7	3	DOUBLE SIDE PUNCH	S	OUT	
34	8	3	SPIN, PARRY	NW	IN	CAT STANCE
35	8	3	LEG CIRCLE, ARM PULL	NW	OUT	SLOW
36	9	3	CROSS STEP, PARRY	NE	IN	CAT STANCE
37	9	3	LEG CIRCLE, ARM PULL	NE	OUT	SLOW
38	0	0	YAME	N	IN, OUT	FINISH

F.11 Chinte

STEP	SS	LS	TECHNIQUE	DIR	BREATH	NOTES
1	0	0	YOI	N	O	READY
2	1	1	HAMMER FIST, RECOVER	E	IN,O,IN	FLOW
3	1	1	HAMMER FIST, RECOVER	W	O,IN	SLOW
4	1	1	SHIFT, LIFT HANDS	E	O	
5	2	1	SHIFT, KNIFE HAND	S	IN	SLOW, LINK
6	2	1	COUNTERPUNCH	S	O	INTO HAND
7	2	1	STEP, KNIFE HAND	S	IN	SLOW, LINK
8	2	1	COUNTERPUNCH	S	O	INTO HAND
9	3	1	STEP, KNIFE HAND	S	IN	SLOW, LINK
10	3	1	RISING ELBOW	S	O	KIAI, LINK
11	3	1	PIVOT, KNIFE HAND	N	IN	
12	3	1	STEP KNIFE HAND	N	O	
13	4	2	FRONTKICK	N	IN	
14	4	2	DOWN & INSIDE BLOCKS	N	O	
15	4	2	STAND, INSIDE SWING	N	IN	
16	4	2	HAMMER FIST BLOCK	N	O	
17	5	2	SHIFT, LOW KNIFE HAND	E	IN,O	SWING ARMS
18	5	2	SHIFT, LOW KNIFE HAND	E	IN,O	SWING ARMS, LINK
19	5	2	SHIFT, INSIDE WEDGE	E	O	
20	6	2	ONE LEG, DOUBLE DOWN	E	IN	SLOW
21	6	2	STEP, ONE KNUCKLE	E	O	STEP BREATH
22	6	2	ONE KNUCKLE	E	O	
23	6	2	INSIDE (FINGERS) BLOCK	E	IN	
24	6	2	2 FINGER THRUST	E	O	
25	7	2	PIVOT, INSIDE BLOCK	W	IN	
26	7	2	2 FINGER THRUST	W	O	
27	8	3	SHIFT, PALM HEEL	S	IN	LINK
28	8	3	2ND PALM HEEL	S	O	
29	8	3	DOUBLE THUMB KNUCKLES	S	IN	
30	8	3	PIVOT, 1 KNUCKLES	N	O	KIAI
31	8	3	STEP, KNIFE HAND	N	IN	
32	9	3	COUNTERPUNCH	N	O	
33	9	3	STEP, KNIFE HAND	N	IN	
34	9	3	COUNTERPUNCH	N	O	
35	10	3	STAND, PALM ON FIST	N	IN	SLOW
36	10	3	HOP BACK (SE)	N	O	FOCUS
37	10	3	HOP BACK (S)	N	IN	LINK
38	10	3	HOP BACK (S)	N	O	
39	0	0	YAME	N	IN,O	STOP

F.12 Enpi

STEP	SS	LS	TECHNIQUE	DIR	BREATH	NOTES
1	0	0	YOI	N	OUT	READY
2	1	1	DROP,BLOCK&PUNCH	N	IN	
3	1	1	RISE & SET HANDS	N	OUT	
4	1	1	TURN, DOWN BLOCK	E	IN	
5	1	1	SHIFT, HOOK PUNCH	N	OUT	
6	2	1	STEP, DOWN BLOCK	N	IN	LINK
7	2	1	RISING COUNTERPUNCH	N	IN	
8	2	1	WRIST HOOK & DRAW	N	OUT	SLOW
9	2	1	LIFT KNEE & ENTER	N	IN	
10	2	1	DROP & PUNCH	N	OUT	STEP BREATH
11	2	1	PULL AWAY & HAMMER	S	OUT	LINK
12	3	1	SHIFT, DOWN BLOCK	S	IN	QUICK
13	3	1	RISING COUNTERPUNCH	S	IN	
14	3	1	WRIST HOOK & DRAW	S	OUT	
15	3	1	LIFT KNEE & ENTER	S	IN	
16	3	1	DROP & PUNCH	S	OUT	
17	3	1	PULL AWAY & HAMMER	N	OUT	LINK
18	4	2	SHIFT, DOWN BLOCK	N	IN,OUT	PAUSE
19	4	2	SWING HAND/FOOT	N	IN	SLOW
20	4	2	SHIFT, ELBOW SMASH	N	OUT	KIAI
21	4	2	STANDING KNIFE HAND	N	IN	
22	4	2	DOUBLE PUNCH	N	OUT,OUT	STEP BREATH
23	5	2	TURN, DOWN BLOCK	W	IN	LINK
24	5	2	RISING PUNCH	W	IN	
25	5	2	STEPPING KNIFE HAND	W	OUT	
26	5	2	SWITCH KNIFE HAND	W	IN	FOOT CHANGE
27	5	2	COUNTERPUNCH	W	OUT	STEP BREATH
28	5	2	STEPPING KNIFE HAND	W	OUT	
29	6	2	TURN, DOWN BLOCK	E	IN	LINK
30	6	2	RISING PUNCH	E	IN	
31	6	2	WRIST HOOK & DRAW	E	OUT	SLOW
32	6	2	LIFT KNEE & ENTER	E	IN	
33	6	2	DROP & PUNCH	E	OUT	STEP BREATH
34	6	2	PULL AWAY & HAMMER	W	OUT	

continued on next page

F.12 Enpi (continued)

STEP	SS	LS	TECHNIQUE	DIR	BREATH	NOTES
35	7	3	SHIFT, DOWN BLOCK	W	IN	PAUSE
36	7	3	RISING PALM HEEL	N	OUT	SLOW
37	7	3	SHIFT, DOUBLE PALMS	N	IN	SLOW
38	7	3	STEP, DOUBLE PALMS	N	OUT	SLOW
39	7	3	STEP, DOUBLE PALMS	N	IN	SLOW
40	8	3	SHIFT, DOWN BLOCK	N	OUT	LINK
41	8	3	SHIFT, DOUBLE GRAB	N	IN	PAUSE
42	8	3	PULL, SPIN, JUMP	N	OUT	KIAI
43	8	3	LAND W/ KNIFE HAND	N	IN	
44	8	3	STEP BACK KNIFE HAND	N	OUT	
45	0	0	YAME	N	IN,OUT	FINISH

F.13 Gankaku

STEP	SS	LS	TECHNIQUE	DIR	BREATH	NOTES
1	0	0	YOI	N	OUT	READY
2	1	1	DOUBLE HAND PARRY	N	IN	
3	1	1	CROSS TWIST GRAB	N	OUT	
4	1	1	HAMMER FIST	N	IN	
5	1	1	COUNTERPUNCH	N	OUT	
6	1	1	PIVOT, STOMP & BLOCK	S	IN,OUT	
7	2	1	TURN, HIGH X BLOCK	N	IN	
8	2	1	PULL DOWN	N	OUT	SLOW
9	2	1	JUMP DOUBLE KICK	N	IN,IN	
10	2	1	LOW X BLOCK	N	OUT	
11	3	1	PIVOT, LOW X BLOCK	S	IN,OUT	
12	3	1	PIVOT, LOW HAMMER FIST	N	IN	
13	3	1	STEP, LOW KNIFE HAND	N	OUT	
14	3	1	STEP, WEDGE BLOCK	N	IN,OUT	SLOW
15	4	2	SHIFT, WEDGE BLOCK	W	IN	SLOW
16	4	2	STAND, DOUBLE DOWN	W	OUT	SLOW
17	4	2	SHIFT, HIGH & LOW	S	IN	
18	4	2	STEP, HIGH & LOW	S	OUT	
19	4	2	PIVOT, HIGH & LOW	S	IN	
20	4	2	DROP, LOW X BLOCK	W	OUT	
21	5	2	INSIDE WEDGE	W	IN	SLOW
22	5	2	STAND, DOUBLE DOWN	W	OUT	SLOW
23	5	2	SWING ELBOWS	W	IN,IN	
24	5	2	PIVOT, INSIDE WEDGE	E	OUT	SLOW
25	6	3	1 LEG, HIGH & LOW	E	IN	SLOW
26	6	3	SETUP HANDS	N	OUT	SLOW
27	6	3	SIDE SNAP & BACKFIST	N	IN	
28	6	3	STEPPING PUNCH	N	OUT	KIAI
29	7	3	1 LEG, HIGH & LOW	W	IN	SLOW
30	7	3	SETUP HANDS	N	OUT	SLOW
31	7	3	SIDE SNAP & BACKFIST	N	IN	
32	7	3	HOOK PUNCH	N	OUT	
33	8	3	1 LEG, HIGH & LOW	W	IN	SLOW
34	8	3	SETUP HANDS	S	OUT	SLOW
35	8	3	SIDE SNAP & BACKFIST	S	IN	
36	8	3	HOOK PUNCH	S	OUT	

continued on next page

F.13 Gankaku (continued)

STEP	SS	LS	TECHNIQUE	DIR	BREATH	NOTES
37	9	3	HIGH BACK HAND BLOCK	N	IN	LINK
38	9	3	RISING ELBOW STRIKE	N	IN	
39	9	3	PUSH DOWN & BACK	N	OUT	SLOW
40	9	3	LIFT & SPIN	E	IN	
41	9	3	SETUP HANDS	S	OUT	SLOW
42	9	3	SIDE SNAP & BACKFIST	S	IN	
43	9	3	STEPPING PUNCH	S	OUT	KIAI
44	0	0	YAME	N	IN,OUT	STOP

F.14 Gojushiho Dai (Useshi)

STEP	SS	LS	TECHNIQUE	DIR	BREATH	NOTES
1	0	0	YOI	N	O	READY
2	1	1	STEPPING BACKFIST	NW	IN,O	SLOW
3	1	1	STEP, WEDGE BLOCK	NE	IN,O	SLOW
4	1	1	CROSS, WEDGE BLOCK	NW	IN,O	SLOW
5	2	1	SHIFT, STANDING KNIFE	NW	IN	SLOW
6	2	1	DOUBLE PUNCH	NW	O,O	STEP BREATH
7	2	1	FRONT KICK + PUNCH	NW	IN,O	STEP IN
8	2	1	SHIFT, STANDING KNIFE	NE	IN	SLOW
9	2	1	DOUBLE PUNCH	NE	O,O	STEP BREATH
10	2	1	FRONT KICK + PUNCH	NE	IN,O	STEP IN
11	3	1	STEP BACK RISING ELBOW	N	IN,O	KIAI
12	3	1	TURN, PULLING KNIFEHAND	S	IN,O	SLOW
13	3	1	DOWN & IN BLOCKS	S	IN	
14	3	1	STEPPING SPEAR HAND	S	O	
15	3	1	DOUBLE SPEARHAND	S	O, O	STEP BREATH
16	4	1	TURN, PULLING KNIFEHAND	N	IN,O	SLOW
17	4	1	DOWN & IN BLOCKS	N	IN	
18	4	1	STEPPING SPEAR HAND	N	O	
19	4	1	DOUBLE SPEARHAND	N	O, O	STEP BREATH
20	5	2	SPIN, LOW RIDGEHANDS	E	IN,O	
21	5	2	STEP ACROSS, HIGH X	E	IN	
22	5	2	STOMP & PULL	E	O	STEP BREATH
23	5	2	LOW RIDGEHAND BLOCKS	W	O	
24	5	2	STEP ACROSS, HIGH X	W	IN	
25	5	2	STOMP & PULL	W	O	
26	6	2	SHIFT, PULLING KNIFEHAND	S	IN,O	
27	6	2	DOWN & IN BLOCKS	S	IN	
28	6	2	STEPPING SPEAR HAND	S	O	
29	6	2	DOUBLE SPEARHAND	S	O,O	STEP BREATH
30	7	2	TURN, KNIFEHAND STRIKE	N	IN,O	
31	7	2	STEP, KNIFEHAND	N	IN	
32	7	2	KNIFEHAND STRIKE	N	O	
33	7	2	STEP, KNIFEHAND	N	IN	
34	7	2	CROSS INSIDE BLOCK	N	O	
35	7	2	FRONT KICK	N	IN	
36	7	2	DROPPING PUNCH	N	O	STEP BREATH
37	7	2	REVERSE HAMMER FIST	S	O	

continued on next page

F.14 Gojushiho Dai (Useshi) (continued)

STEP	SS	LS	TECHNIQUE	DIR	BREATH	NOTES
38	8	2	PULLING KNIFEHAND	S	IN,O	SLOW
39	8	2	DOWN & IN BLOCKS	S	IN	
40	8	2	STEPPING SPEAR HAND	S	O	
41	8	2	DOUBLE SPEARHAND	S	O,O	STEP BREATH
42	9	3	SPIN, LOW RIDGEHAND	W	IN,O	
43	9	3	STEP ACROSS, PARRY	W	IN	
44	9	3	STOMP & PUNCH	W	O	
45	9	3	LOW RIDGEHAND BLOCK	E	O	STEP BREATH
46	9	3	STEP ACROSS, PARRY	E	IN	
47	9	3	STOMP & PUNCH	E	O	
48	10	3	STEPPING BACKFIST	N	IN,O	SLOW
49	10	3	STEP BACK HAMMER FIST	N	IN	LINK
50	10	3	STEPPING PUNCH	N	O	
51	11	3	STAND, SCISSORS PUNCH	W	IN	LINK
52	11	3	BACK DOUBLE KNUCKLES	W	O	LINK
53	11	3	STANDING, SIDE ELBOWS	W	IN	
54	11	3	TURN, ELBOW WEDGE	S	O	SLOW
55	12	3	STEP, 2 ARM UP CIRCLE	S	IN	
56	12	3	DOUBLE LOW WEDGE	S	O	
57	12	3	RISING WRISTS	S	IN	
58	12	3	DOUBLE BOTTOM WRIST	S	O	KIAI
59	12	3	TURN, PULLING KNIFEHAND	N	IN,O	SLOW
60	0	0	YAME	N	IN,O	STOP

F.15 Gojushiho Sho (Hotaku)

STEP	SS	LS	TECHNIQUE	DIR	BREATH	NOTES
1	0	0	YOI	N	O	READY
2	1	1	STEPPING BACKFIST	NW	IN,O	SLOW
3	1	1	STEP, 2 HAND PUNCH	NE	IN,O	SLOW
4	1	1	STEP, 2 HAND PUNCH	NW	IN,O	SLOW
5	1	1	SHIFT, STANDING KNIFE	NW	IN	SLOW
6	1	1	DOUBLE PUNCH	NW	O,O	STEP BREATH
7	1	1	FRONT KICK+CTR. PUNCH	NW	IN,O	IN PLACE
8	1	1	SHIFT, STANDING KNIFE	NE	IN	SLOW
9	1	1	DOUBLE PUNCH	NE	O,O	STEP BREATH
10	1	1	FRONT KICK+CTR. PUNCH	NE	IN,O	IN PLACE
11	2	1	STEPPING ELBOW STRIKE	N	IN	
12	2	1	TURN, CROSS THROW	S	O	
13	2	1	TURN, WRIST BLOCK	S	IN	SLOW, LINK
14	2	1	DOWN & UP PARRY	S	IN	
15	2	1	SLIDING FINGER STRIKE	S	O	
16	2	1	DOUBLE FINGER STRIKES	S	O,O	STEP BREATH
17	3	1	DOWN & UP PARRY	N	IN	
18	3	1	SLIDING FINGER STRIKE	N	O	
19	3	1	DOUBLE FINGER STRIKES	N	O,O	STEP BREATH
20	4	2	SPIN, LOW RIDGEHAND	E	IN,O	
21	4	2	STEP ACROSS, HIGH GRIP	E	IN	
22	4	2	STOMP & THROW	E	O	STEP BREATH
23	4	2	LOW RIDGEHAND BLOCK	W	O	
24	4	2	STEP ACROSS, HIGH GRIP	W	IN	
25	4	2	STOMP & THROW	W	O	
26	5	2	RISING WRIST BLOCK	S	IN	SLOW, LINK
27	5	2	DOWN & UP PARRY	S	IN	
28	5	2	SLIDING FINGER STRIKE	S	O	
29	5	2	DOUBLE FINGER STRIKES	S	O,O	STEP BREATH
30	6	2	TURN, KNIFEHAND STRIKE	N	IN,O	MIDDLE
31	6	2	STEP, BACKFIST	N	IN	SLOW
32	6	2	KNIFEHAND STRIKE	N	O	MIDDLE
33	6	2	STEP, BACKFIST	N	IN	
34	6	2	STEP, DOWN & UP BEAKS	N	O	
35	6	2	FRONT KICK	N	IN	KEEP LEG UP
36	6	2	BLOCK W/ COUNTERPUNCH	N	O	STEP BREATH
37	6	2	DROP AWAY HAMMER FIST	S	O	WITH HIGH ELBOW

continued on next page

F.15 Gojushiho Sho (Hotaku) (continued)

STEP	SS	LS	TECHNIQUE	DIR	BREATH	NOTES
38	7	2	RISING WRIST BLOCK	S	IN	SLOW, LINK
39	7	2	DOWN & UP PARRY	S	IN	
40	7	2	SLIDING FINGER STRIKE	S	O	
41	7	2	DOUBLE FINGER STRIKES	S	O,O	LINKED
42	8	3	SPIN, LOW RIDGEHAND	W	IN,O	
43	8	3	STEP ACROSS, PARRY	W	IN	
44	8	3	STOMP & SPEAR	W	O	
45	8	3	LOW RIDGEHAND BLOCK	E	O	STEP BREATH
46	8	3	STEP ACROSS, PARRY	E	IN	
47	8	3	STOMP & SPEAR	E	O	
48	9	3	STEPPING BACKFIST	N	IN,O	SLOW
49	9	3	STEP BACK HAMMER FIST	N	IN	
50	9	3	STEPPING PUNCH	N	O	KIAI
51	9	3	STAND, LIFT ELBOWS	W	IN	
52	9	3	BEHIND DOUBLE KNUCKLES	W	O	
53	9	3	STANDING, HIGH ELBOWS	W	IN	
54	9	3	TURN, ELBOW WEDGE	S	O	SLOW
55	10	3	STEP, 2 ARM UP CIRCLE	S	IN	
56	10	3	DOUBLE LOW WEDGE	S	O	
57	10	3	RISING WRISTS	S	IN	
58	10	3	DOUBLE FINGER STABS	S	O	KIAI
59	10	3	TURN, RISING WRIST	N	IN,O	SLOW
60	0	0	YAME	N	IN,O	STOP

F.16 Hangetsu

STEP	SS	LS	TECHNIQUE	DIR	BREATH	NOTES
1	0	0	YOI	N	OUT	READY
2	1	1	STEP INSIDE BLOCK	N	IN	SLOW
3	1	1	COUNTERPUNCH	N	OUT	SLOW
4	1	1	STEP INSIDE BLOCK	N	IN	SLOW
5	1	1	COUNTERPUNCH	N	OUT	SLOW
6	1	1	STEP INSIDE BLOCK	N	IN	SLOW
7	1	1	COUNTERPUNCH	N	OUT	SLOW
8	2	1	EXTEND ONE KNUCKLES	N	IN	SLOW
9	2	1	INWARD THUMBS	N	OUT	SLOW
10	2	1	EXTEND ARMS	N	IN	LINK,SLOW
11	2	1	DOUBLE HIGH BLOCKS	N	IN	SLOW
12	2	1	DOUBLE DOWN BLOCKS	N	OUT, IN	PAUSE
13	3	2	SPIN, MIDDLE & LOW	S	OUT	KIAI,LINK
14	3	2	WRIST HOOK	S	OUT	SLOW
15	3	2	STEP, MIDDLE & LOW	S	IN	QUICK
16	3	2	WRIST HOOK	S	OUT	SLOW
17	3	2	STEP, MIDDLE & LOW	S	IN	QUICK
18	3	2	WRIST HOOK	S	OUT	SLOW
19	4	2	SHIFT, INSIDE BLOCK	W	IN	QUICK
20	4	2	DOUBLE PUNCH	W	OUT,OUT	STEP BREATH
21	4	2	SPIN, INSIDE BLOCK	E	IN	
22	4	2	DOUBLE PUNCH	E	OUT,OUT	STEP BREATH
23	4	2	TURN, INSIDE BLOCK	S	IN	
24	4	2	DOUBLE PUNCH	S	OUT,OUT	STEP BREATH
25	5	3	TURN, SWING ARM/LEG	N	IN,OUT	SLOW
26	5	3	CROSS STEP	N	NONE	SLOW
27	5	3	FRONT KICK	N	IN	
28	5	3	DOWN BLOCK	N	OUT	STEP BREATH
29	5	3	COUNTERPUNCH	N	OUT	
30	5	3	RISING BLOCK	N	IN	
31	5	3	TURN	S	OUT	SLOW,LINK
32	6	3	SWING ARM/LEG	S	IN,OUT	SLOW
33	6	3	CROSS STEP	S	NONE	SLOW
34	6	3	FRONT KICK	S	IN	
35	6	3	DOWN BLOCK	S	OUT	STEP BREATH
36	6	3	COUNTERPUNCH	S	OUT	
37	6	3	RISING BLOCK	S	IN	
38	6	3	TURN	N	OUT	SLOW,LINK

continued on next page

F.16 Hangetsu (continued)

STEP	SS	LS	TECHNIQUE	DIR	BREATH	NOTES
39	7	3	SWING ARM/LEG	N	IN,OUT	SLOW
40	7	3	CRESCENT KICK	N	IN	
41	7	3	DOWN PUNCH	N	OUT	KIAI
42	7	3	PULL BACK	N	IN	
43	7	3	PALM HEEL PUSH	N	OUT	SLOW
44	0	0	YAME	N	IN,OUT	FINISH

F.17 Ji'in

STEP	SS	LS	TECHNIQUE	DIR	BREATH	NOTES
1	0	0	YOI	N	O	READY
2	1	1	IN & DOWN BLOCKS	N	IN	LEFT HAND HIGH
3	1	1	STEP SIDE, HIGH & LOW	W	O	LINK
4	1	1	SHIFT, HIGH & LOW	E	O	
5	2	1	SHIFT, PARRY UP BLOCK	NW	IN	
6	2	1	STEPPING PUNCH	NW	O	
7	2	1	SHIFT, PARRY UP BLOCK	NE	IN	
8	2	1	STEPPING PUNCH	NE	O	
9	3	1	SHIFT, DOWN BLOCK	N	IN	
10	3	1	STEP, KNIFEHAND STRIKE	N	O	
11	3	1	STEP, KNIFEHAND STRIKE	N	IN	LINK
12	3	1	STEP, KNIFEHAND STRIKE	N	O	KIAI
13	4	2	TURN, WEDGE BLOCK	SE	IN,O	SLOW
14	4	2	STEPPING KICK	SE	IN	
15	4	2	DOUBLE PUNCH	SE	O,O	STEP BREATH
16	4	2	IN & DOWN BLOCK	SE	O	
17	5	2	SHIFT, WEDGE BLOCK	SW	IN,O	SLOW
18	5	2	STEPPING KICK	SW	IN	
19	5	2	DOUBLE PUNCH	SW	O,O	
20	5	2	IN & DOWN BLOCK	SW	O	
21	6	3	PIVOT, HAMMER FIST	S	IN	
22	6	3	PIVOT, HAMMER FIST	S	O	LINK
23	6	3	STEP, HAMMER FIST	S	O	
24	7	3	STEP, KNIFEHAND PUSH	SE	IN	SLOW
25	7	3	PUNCH,PUNCH	SE	O,O	
26	7	3	KICK, PUNCH	SE	IN,O	LINK
27	7	3	IN & DOWN BLOCK	SE	O	
28	8	3	PIVOT, IN & DOWN BLOCK	N	IN	
29	8	3	DOWN BLOCK	N	O	SLOW
30	8	3	INSIDE WEDGE	N	IN	
31	8	3	PUNCH,PUNCH	N	O,O	STEP BREATH KIAI
32	0	0	YAME	N	IN,O	STOP

F.18 Jion

STEP	SS	LS	TECHNIQUE	DIR	BREATH	NOTES
1	0	0	YOI	N	O	READY
2	1	1	IN & DOWNBLOCK	N	IN	RIGHT HAND HIGH
3	1	1	STEP, WEDGE BLOCK	NW	O	
4	1	1	KICK, PUNCH	NW	IN, O	STEP BREATH
5	1	1	DOUBLE PUNCH	NW	O,O	
6	2	1	SHIFT, WEDGE BLOCK	NE	IN,O	
7	2	1	KICK, PUNCH	NE	IN,O	STEP BREATH
8	2	1	DOUBLE PUNCH	NE	O,O	
9	3	1	SHIFT UP BLOCK, PUNCH	N	IN,O	
10	3	1	STEP UP BLOCK, PUNCH	N	IN,O	
11	3	1	STEP UP BLOCK	N	IN	LINK
12	3	1	STEPPING PUNCH	N	O	KIAI
13	4	1	270, HIGH & LOW	E	IN	
14	4	1	SHIFT, HOOK PUNCH	E	O	
15	4	1	TURN, HIGH & LOW	W	IN	
16	4	1	SHIFT, HOOK PUNCH	W	O	
17	5	2	SHIFT, DOWN BLOCK	S	IN	
18	5	2	STEP, PALM HEEL	S	O	
19	5	2	STEP, PALM HEEL	S	IN	LINK
20	5	2	STEP, PALM HEEL	S	O	
21	6	2	270, HIGH & LOW	W	IN	
22	6	2	HIGH AUGMENTED BL	W	O	
23	6	2	SHIFT, HIGH & LOW	E	IN	
24	6	2	HIGH AUGMENTED BL	E	O	
25	6	2	OPEN TO SIDES	N	IN,O	
26	7	2	LIFT LEG, LOW X-BLOCK	N	IN,O	
27	7	2	PULLING LOW WEDGE	N	IN	
28	7	2	STEP, INNER WEDGE	N	O	
29	7	2	STEP, UP X BLOCK	N	IN	LINK
30	7	2	RT STANDING FIST	N	O	QUICK
31	7	2	PULL UPBLOCK W/ PUNCH	N	IN	LINK
32	7	2	INVERTED PUNCH	N	O	(KIAI OPTIONAL)
33	8	3	SPIN, INSIDE BLOCK	E	IN	
34	8	3	STEP PUNCH	E	O	
35	8	3	SPIN, INSIDE BLOCK	W	IN	
36	8	3	STEP PUNCH	W	O	

continued on next page

F.18 Jion (continued)

STEP	SS	LS	TECHNIQUE	DIR	BREATH	NOTES
37	9	3	DOWN BLOCK	S	IN	
38	9	3	STOMP	S	O	
39	9	3	STOMP	S	IN	
40	9	3	STOMP	S	O	
41	10	3	SPIN, PARRY	W	IN	
42	10	3	SIDE PUNCH	W	O	SLOW (ALT. HAMMER)
43	10	3	PARRY	E	IN	
44	10	3	SLIDE SIDE PUNCH	E	O	KIAI, SLOW
45	0	0	YAME	N	IN,O	STOP

F.19 Jutte

STEP	SS	LS	TECHNIQUE	DIR	BREATH	NOTES
1	0	0	YOI	N	OUT	READY
2	1	1	PALM HEEL, HOOKING PALM	N	IN,OUT	SLOW
3	1	1	STEP, PALM HEELS	W	IN,OUT	SLOW
4	1	1	CROSS CLAMP	E	IN	LINK
5	1	1	SHIFT, RIDGE HAND	E	OUT	
6	2	1	SHIFT, PALM HEEL	N	IN,OUT	
7	2	1	STEP, PALM HEEL	N	IN	
8	2	1	STEP, PALM HEEL	N	OUT	
9	3	1	CROSS STEP, HIGH X	S	IN	LINK
10	3	1	DOUBLE DOWN BLOCK	S	OUT	LINK
11	3	1	CLOSE STEP, HIGH X	S	IN	LINK
12	3	1	DOUBLE HIGH BLOCK	W	OUT	
13	4	2	CRESCENT KICK	N	IN	
14	4	2	STOMP, HIGH HAMMER	N	OUT	
15	4	2	CRESCENT KICK	N	IN	
16	4	2	STOMP, HIGH HAMMER	N	OUT	
17	4	2	CRESCENT KICK	N	IN	
18	4	2	STOMP, HIGH HAMMER	N	OUT	KIAI
19	5	2	STAND, DOUBLE DOWN	E	IN,OUT	SLOW
20	5	2	SHIFT, HIGH KNIFEHAND	S	IN	LINK
21	5	2	DOUBLE PALM THRUST	S	OUT	
22	5	2	TURN HANDS, PULL	S	IN	STAND 1 LEG
23	5	2	DOUBLE PALM THRUST	S	OUT	
24	5	2	TURN HANDS, PULL	S	IN	STAND 1 LEG
25	5	2	DOUBLE PALM THRUST	S	OUT	
26	6	3	PIVOT, HIGH & LOW	W	IN	LINK
27	6	3	SHIFT, HIGH & LOW	E	OUT	
28	7	3	PARRY W/ UP BLOCK	N	IN	
29	7	3	STEP UP BLOCK	N	OUT	LINK
30	7	3	PIVOT UP BLOCK	S	IN	
31	7	3	STEP UP BLOCK	S	OUT	KIAI
32	0	0	PIVOT, YAME	N	IN,OUT	STOP

F.20 Kanku Dai

STEP	SS	LS	TECHNIQUE	DIR	BREATH	NOTES
1	0	0	YOI	N	OUT	READY
2	1	1	RAISE HANDS	N	IN	SLOW
3	1	1	OPEN, LOW KNIFEHAND	N	OUT	QUICK,SLOW
4	1	1	HIGH BACKHAND	W	IN	LINK
5	1	1	HIGH BACKHAND	E	OUT	
6	2	1	STANDING KNIFEHAND	N	IN	SLOW
7	2	1	PUNCH	N	OUT	STEP BREATH
8	2	1	INSIDE BLOCK	N	OUT	
9	2	1	WAIT, PUNCH	N	IN,OUT	STEP BREATH
10	2	1	INSIDE BLOCK	N	OUT	
11	3	1	SIDE SNAP,BACKFIST	S	IN	
12	3	1	KNIFEHAND	N	OUT	
13	3	1	KNIFEHAND	N	IN	
14	3	1	KNIFEHAND	N	OUT	LINK
15	3	1	PARRY, SPEARHAND	N	OUT	KIAI
16	4	1	SPIN, STRIKE	S	IN,OUT	WITH BLOCK
17	4	1	KICK	S	IN	
18	4	1	SPIN, LOW & HIGH	N	OUT	STEP BREATH
19	4	1	PARRY, LOW PALMHEEL	N	OUT	
20	4	1	PULL BACK, DOWN BLOCK	N	IN,OUT	SLOW
21	5	1	REACH, STRIKE	N	IN,OUT	WITH BLOCK
22	5	1	KICK	N	IN	
23	5	1	SPIN, LOW & HIGH	S	OUT	STEP BREATH
24	5	1	PARRY, LOW PALMHEEL	S	OUT	
25	5	1	PULL BACK, DOWN BLOCK	S	IN,OUT	
26	6	2	SIDE SNAP, BACKFIST	E	IN	
27	6	2	REACH, ELBOW SMASH	E	OUT	
28	6	2	SIDE SNAP, BACKFIST	W	IN	
29	6	2	REACH, ELBOW SMASH	W	OUT	
30	7	2	KNIFEHAND	E	IN	
31	7	2	KNIFEHAND	SE	OUT	
32	7	2	KNIFEHAND	W	IN	
33	7	2	KNIFEHAND	SW	OUT	
34	8	2	REACH, STRIKE	S	IN,OUT	WITH BLOCK
35	8	2	KICK	S	IN	
36	8	2	BACKFIST	S	OUT	
37	8	2	INSIDE BLOCK	S	IN	
38	8	2	DOUBLE PUNCH	S	OUT,OUT	STEP BREATH

continued on next page

F.20 Kanku Dai (continued)

STEP	SS	LS	TECHNIQUE	DIR	BREATH	NOTES
39	9	2	SPIN, LUNGE THRUST	N	IN	
40	9	2	DROP	N	OUT	
41	9	2	SPIN, LOW KNIFEHAND	S	IN	
42	9	2	STEP, KNIFEHAND	S	OUT	
43	10	3	SPIN, INSIDE BLOCK	W	IN	
44	10	3	COUNTERPUNCH	W	OUT	
45	10	3	TURN, INSIDE BLOCK	E	IN	
46	10	3	DOUBLE PUNCH	E	OUT,OUT	STEP BREATH
47	10	3	SIDE SNAP W/ BACKFIST	S	IN	
48	10	3	KNIFEHAND	N	OUT	
49	11	3	PARRY, SPEARHAND	N	IN,OUT	STEPPING
50	11	3	SPIN, BACKFIST	E	IN	LINK
51	11	3	SLIDE, HAMMER FIST	E	OUT	
52	11	3	ELBOW SMASH	E	IN	
53	11	3	SET HANDS	E	OUT	STEP BREATH
54	11	3	DOWN BLOCK	E	OUT	
55	12	3	"GREAT WHEEL" STOMP	W	IN,OUT	STEP BREATH
56	12	3	DROPPING PUNCH	W	OUT	
57	12	3	LIFTING X BLOCK	W	IN	
58	12	3	TURN 270, PULL DOWN	S	OUT	
59	13	3	DOUBLE FLYING KICK	S	IN	
60	13	3	BACKFIST	S	OUT	KIAI
61	13	3	SPIN, LOW INSIDE WEDGE	N	IN	
62	13	3	DOUBLE LIFT	N	OUT	
63	0	0	YAME	N	IN,OUT	STOP

F.21 Kanku Sho

STEP	SS	LS	TECHNIQUE	DIR	BREATH	NOTES
1	0	0	YOI	N	OUT	READY
2	1	1	AUGMENTED BLOCK	W	IN	
3	1	1	AUGMENTED BLOCK	E	OUT	LINK
4	1	1	AUGMENTED BLOCK	N	OUT,IN	PAUSE
5	2	1	STEP PUNCH,BLOCK	N	OUT,IN	
6	2	1	STEP PUNCH,BLOCK	N	OUT,IN	LINK
7	2	1	STEP PUNCH	N	OUT	KIAI
8	3	1	TURN, SWING HANDS	S	IN	LINK
9	3	1	WRIST BREAK	S	OUT	
10	3	1	PULL,FRONT KICK	S	IN	
11	3	1	BACKFIST STRIKE	S	OUT	
12	3	1	INSIDE BLOCK	S	IN	
13	3	1	DOUBLE PUNCH	S	OUT,OUT	STEP BREATH
14	3	1	TURN & THROW	N	IN	
15	3	1	DOWN BLOCK	N	OUT	SLOW
16	4	1	SHIFT, SWING HANDS	N	IN	LINK
17	4	1	WRIST BREAK	N	OUT	
18	4	1	PULL,FRONT KICK	N	IN	
19	4	1	BACKFIST STRIKE	N	OUT	
20	4	1	INSIDE BLOCK	N	IN	
21	4	1	DOUBLE PUNCH	N	OUT,OUT	STEP BREATH
22	4	1	TURN & THROW	S	IN	
23	4	1	DOWN BLOCK	S	OUT	SLOW
24	5	2	HIGH & LOW BLOCKS	E	IN	
25	5	2	DOUBLE SIDE PUNCH	E	OUT	
26	5	2	HIGH & LOW BLOCKS	W	IN	
27	5	2	DOUBLE SIDE PUNCH	W	OUT	
28	5	2	SHIFT, GRAB/TURN STAFF	S	IN	
29	5	2	THRUST STAFF	S	OUT	
30	5	2	JUMP SPIN, KNIFEHAND	S	IN,OUT	(KIAI OPTIONAL)
31	6	2	SIDE SNAP,ELBOW	E	IN,OUT	
32	6	2	SIDE SNAP,ELBOW	W	IN,OUT	
33	7	2	SHIFT, SWING HANDS	S	IN	
34	7	2	WRIST BREAK	S	OUT	
35	7	2	PULL,FRONT KICK	S	IN	
36	7	2	BACKFIST STRIKE	S	OUT	
37	7	2	INSIDE BLOCK	S	IN	
38	7	2	DOUBLE PUNCH	S	OUT,OUT	STEP BREATH

continued on next page

F.21 Kanku Sho (continued)

STEP	SS	LS	TECHNIQUE	DIR	BREATH	NOTES
39	8	3	BACK HAND BEHIND	S	IN	SLOW
40	8	3	JUMP, SPIN, DROP	S	OUT	QUICK LINK
41	8	3	JUMP KNIFEHAND	S	IN	
42	8	3	KNIFEHAND BLOCK	S	OUT	
43	9	3	SPIN, INSIDE BLOCK	W	IN	
44	9	3	STEPPING PUNCH	W	OUT	
45	9	3	TURN, INSIDE BLOCK	E	IN	
46	9	3	STEPPING PUNCH	E	OUT	KIAI
47	0	0	YAME	N	IN,OUT	STOP

F.22 Meikyo

STEP	SS	LS	TECHNIQUE	DIR	BREATH	NOTES
1	0	0	YOI	N	OUT	READY
2	1	1	CIRCLE HANDS & SET	N	IN,OUT	SLOW
3	1	1	LIFT, INSIDE WEDGE	N	IN,OUT	SLOW
4	2	1	SHIFT, DOWN BLOCK	NW	IN	
5	2	1	STEPPING PUNCH	NW	OUT	
6	2	1	SHIFT, DOWN BLOCK	NE	IN	
7	2	1	STEPPING PUNCH	NE	OUT	
8	2	1	SHIFT STEP, PARRY	N	IN	STAFF, 2 HANDS
9	2	1	2-HAND THRUST	N	OUT	STEP BREATH
10	2	1	PIVOT, TWIST HANDS	S	OUT	
11	2	1	CIRCLE HANDS & SET	S	IN,OUT	
12	3	2	SHIFT, INSIDE BLOCK	SE	IN	
13	3	2	STEPPING PUNCH	SE	OUT	
14	3	2	SHIFT, INSIDE BLOCK	SW	IN	
15	3	2	STEPPING PUNCH	SW	OUT	
16	3	2	SHIFT STEP, PARRY	S	IN	STAFF, 2 HANDS
17	3	2	2-HAND THRUST	S	OUT	
18	3	2	PIVOT, TWIST HANDS	N	OUT	
19	3	2	CIRCLE HANDS & SET	N	IN,OUT	
20	4	2	SHIFT, RISING BLOCK	NW	IN	
21	4	2	STEPPING PUNCH	NW	OUT	
22	4	2	SHIFT, RISING BLOCK	NE	IN	
23	4	2	STEPPING PUNCH	NE	OUT	STEP BREATH
24	5	3	SHIFT, HAMMER FIST	N	IN	
25	5	3	CRESCENT KICK	N	OUT	KIAI, LINK
26	5	3	DOUBLE DOWN WEDGE	N	OUT	
27	6	3	2 FISTS UP	N	IN	
28	6	3	STEP, 2 FISTS UP	N	OUT	
29	6	3	MOVING IN HIGH X	N	IN	FEET MOVING
30	6	3	LOWER WEDGE	N	OUT	
31	6	3	STEP, INSIDE WEDGE	N	IN	
32	6	3	2 FIST INV. PUNCHES	N	OUT	
33	7	3	PIVOT, RISING BLOCK	S	IN	
34	7	3	JUMPING PIVOT, ELBOW	N	OUT	KIAI
35	7	3	SPIN, KNIFEHAND BLOCK	N	IN	
36	7	3	STEP BACK, KNIFEHAND	N	OUT	
37	0	0	YAME	N	IN,OUT	STOP

F.23 Nijushiho

STEP	SS	LS	TECHNIQUE	DIR	BREATH	NOTES
1	0	0	YOI	N	OUT	READY
2	1	1	SHIFT, PALM HELL PRESS	N	IN	
3	1	1	COUNTERPUNCH	N	OUT	STEP BREATH
4	1	1	RISING ELBOW STRIKE	N	OUT	
5	2	1	PIVOT, EYE RAKE	S	IN	
6	2	1	DOUBLE PUNCH	S	OUT	
7	2	1	DOUBLE PULL	S	IN	
8	2	1	WEDGE BLOCK	S	OUT	
9	3	1	TURN, RISING BLOCK	E	IN	
10	3	1	ELBOW STRIKE	E	OUT	
11	4	2	STANDING KNIFEHAND	W	IN	SLOW
12	4	2	SIDE THRUST KICK	W	OUT	STEP BREATH
13	4	2	HOOK PUNCH	W	OUT	
14	4	2	STANDING KNIFEHAND	E	IN	SLOW
15	4	2	SIDE THRUST KICK	E	OUT	STEP BREATH
16	4	2	HOOK PUNCH	E	OUT	
17	5	2	PULL IN, HOOK PALM	SE	IN	QUICK
18	5	2	DOUBLE PALM HEELS	SE	OUT	SLOW
19	5	2	PIVOT, RIDGE & KNIFE	NW	IN	LINK
20	5	2	RISING BACK HAND	NW	OUT	KIAI
21	5	2	DROP, LEG TACKLE	NW	IN	
22	5	2	LOW DOUBLE PUNCH	NW	OUT	
23	6	3	TURN, BACK HAND	SE	IN	SLOW
24	6	3	STEP, RISING ELBOW	SE	OUT	
25	6	3	PARRY & GRAB	SE	IN	SLIDE IN
26	6	3	DOWN BLOCK	SE	OUT	
27	7	3	TURN, BACK HAND	NW	IN	SLOW
28	7	3	STEP, ELBOW SMASH	NW	OUT	STEP BREATH
29	7	3	DOWN HAMMER	NW	OUT	
30	8	3	STEP, BACK HAND	SW	IN	SLOW
31	8	3	STEP, RISING ELBOW	SW	OUT	
32	8	3	PARRY & GRAB	SW	IN	SLIDE IN
33	8	3	DOWN BLOCK	SW	OUT	
34	9	3	PIVOT, EYE RAKE	N	IN	
35	9	3	DOUBLE PUNCH	N	OUT	KIAI
36	9	3	ROUNDHOUSE BLOCK	N	IN,OUT	SLOW
37	0	0	YAME	N	IN,OUT	STOP

F.24 Sochin

STEP	SS	LS	TECHNIQUE	DIR	BREATH	NOTES
1	0	0	YOI	N	OUT	READY
2	1	1	UP & DOWN BLOCK	N	IN,OUT	
3	1	1	COUNTER KNIFEHAND	N	IN	
4	1	1	DOUBLE PUNCH	N	OUT,OUT	STEP BREATH
5	2	1	TURN, HIGH & LOW	W	IN	
6	2	1	UP & DOWN BLOCK	W	OUT	
7	2	1	COUNTER KNIFEHAND	W	IN	
8	2	1	DOUBLE PUNCH	W	OUT,OUT	STEP BREATH
9	3	1	TURN, HIGH & LOW	E	IN	
10	3	1	UP & DOWN BLOCK	E	OUT	
11	3	1	COUNTER KNIFEHAND	E	IN	
12	3	1	DOUBLE PUNCH	E	OUT,OUT	STEP BREATH
13	4	2	TURN, SIDE SNAP	W	IN	W/ BACKFIST
14	4	2	REACH, ELBOW SMASH	W	OUT	
15	4	2	TURN, SIDE SNAP	E	IN	W/ BACKFIST
16	4	2	REACH, ELBOW SMASH	E	OUT	
17	5	2	SPIN, KNIFEHAND	W	IN	
18	5	2	STEP, KNIFEHAND	SW	OUT	
19	5	2	TURN, KNIFEHAND	E	IN	
20	5	2	STEP, KNIFEHAND	SE	OUT	
21	6	2	SHIFT, KNIFEHAND	S	IN	
22	6	2	STEP, KNIFEHAND	S	OUT	
23	6	2	SHUFFLE, INV. SPEAR	S	IN	LINK
24	6	2	FR. LEG FR. KICK	S	IN	ADVANCING
25	6	2	FR. KICK W/ BACKFIST	S	OUT	STEP BREATH
26	6	2	BACKFIST W/ BLOCK	S	OUT	KIAI
27	7	3	SPIN, CRESCENT KICK	N	IN	
28	7	3	UP & DOWN BLOCK	N	OUT	
29	7	3	STEP, INSIDE BLOCK	NW	IN	
30	7	3	STEPPING PUNCH	NW	OUT	
31	7	3	SHIFT, INSIDE BLOCK	NE	IN	
32	7	3	STEPPING PUNCH	NE	OUT	
33	8	3	SHIFT, INSIDE BLOCK	N	IN	LINK
34	8	3	REV. INSIDE BLOCK	N	IN	
35	8	3	FRONT KICK	N	OUT	IN PLACE
36	8	3	DRAW HAND W/ REACH	N	IN	SLOW
37	8	3	DOUBLE PUNCH	N	OUT,OUT	KIAI
38	0	0	YAME	N	IN,OUT	FINISH

F.25 Unsu

STEP	SS	LS	TECHNIQUE	DIR	BREATH	NOTES
1	0	0	YOI	N	OUT	READY
2	1	1	CIRCLE ARMS TO SIDES	N	IN,OUT	SLOW (YOI #2)
3	1	1	RAISE PALMS	N	IN	SLOW
4	1	1	HAND PARRIES TO SIDE	N	OUT	SLOW
5	2	1	DOUBLE WRIST PARRY	N	IN	RT FT FWD
6	2	1	FINGER THRUST	N	OUT	
7	2	1	STEP, CIRCLE FOOT	N	IN	SLOW
8	2	1	FINGER THRUST	N	OUT	
9	2	1	STEP, CIRCLE FOOT	N	IN	SLOW
10	2	1	FINGER THRUST	N	OUT	
11	3	1	SHIFT, KNIFEHAND	W	IN	
12	3	1	COUNTERPUNCH	W	OUT	
13	3	1	TURN, KNIFEHAND	E	IN	
14	3	1	COUNTERPUNCH	E	OUT	
15	3	1	SHIFT, KNIFEHAND	N	IN	
16	3	1	COUNTERPUNCH	N	OUT	
17	3	1	TURN, KNIFEHAND	S	IN	
18	3	1	COUNTERPUNCH	S	OUT	
19	4	1	DROP, ROUND KICK	S	IN	
20	4	1	SWITCH, ROUND KICK	S	OUT	
21	4	1	STAND, KNIFEHANDS	W	IN	SLOW
22	4	1	SWITCH, WRIST & KNIFE	N	OUT	PAUSE
23	5	2	SWITCH, WRIST & KNIFE	N	IN	LINK
24	5	2	RIDGEHAND	N	OUT	
25	5	2	FRONTKICK	N	IN	
26	5	2	PIVOT, CROSS BLOCK	S	OUT	LINK
27	5	2	COUNTERPUNCH	S	OUT	
28	6	2	PIVOT, RIDGEHAND	N	IN,OUT	LINK
29	6	2	FRONTKICK	N	IN	
30	6	2	PIVOT, CROSS BLOCK	S	OUT	
31	6	2	COUNTERPUNCH	S	OUT	
32	6	2	STAND, DOUBLE DOWN	S	IN,OUT	SLOW

continued on next page

F.25 Unsu (continued)

STEP	SS	LS	TECHNIQUE	DIR	BREATH	NOTES
33	7	2	STEP, HIGH & LOW WRIST	SE	IN	
34	7	2	STEP, PUNCH DOWN	SE	OUT	
35	7	2	PIVOT, PUNCH	NW	IN	LINK
36	7	2	PIVOT, PUNCH	SE	OUT	
37	7	2	PIVOT, KNIFEHAND	NW	IN	SLOW
38	7	2	RISING PALMHEEL GRAB	NW	OUT	
39	7	2	FRONT THRUST HEEL KICK	NW	IN,OUT	KIAI
40	7	2	COUNTERPUNCH	NW	IN	LINK
41	7	2	STRAIGHT PUNCH	NW	OUT	
42	8	3	PIVOT STEP, DOWNBLOCK	S	IN,OUT	
43	8	3	RISING INSIDE BLOCK	N	IN	(KNIFEHAND)
44	8	3	PIVOT STEP, DOWNBLOCK	S	OUT	(KNIFEHAND)
45	8	3	RISING INSIDE BLOCK	N	IN	
46	8	3	HOOK PUNCH	N	OUT	
47	8	3	PIVOT JUMP, CRESCENT	N	IN	
48	8	3	DROP	S	OUT	RT FT FWD
49	9	3	STEP UP, ROUND BLOCK	S	IN,OUT	SLOW
50	9	3	STEP UP, ROUND BLOCK	S	IN,OUT	SLOW
51	9	3	PIVOT, UPBLOCK	N	IN	
52	9	3	RT. HAND COUNTERPUNCH	N	OUT	KIAI
53	9	3	PULL BACK, DOUBLE DOWN	N	IN,OUT	SLOW
54	0	0	YAME	N	IN,OUT	STOP

F.26 Wankan

STEP	SS	LS	TECHNIQUE	DIR	BREATH	NOTES
1	0	0	YOI	N	OUT	READY
2	1	1	CROSS STEP, WEDGE	NW	IN,OUT	SLOW
3	1	1	CROSS STEP, WEDGE	NE	IN,OUT	SLOW
4	2	1	LIFT KNEE & HANDS	N	IN	
5	2	1	RUN	N	OUT	
6	2	1	RUN	N	OUT	
7	2	1	RUN, CROSS KNIFEHAND	N	IN	SLOW
8	2	1	RT PUNCH, LF PUNCH	N	OUT,OUT	
9	3	2	SHIFT, CROSS THROW	W	IN	
10	3	2	STEP, CROSS KNIFEHAND	W	OUT	SLOW
11	3	2	PUNCH,PUNCH	W	IN,OUT	LINK
12	4	2	TURN, CROSS THROW	E	IN	
13	4	2	STEP, CROSS KNIFEHAND	E	OUT	SLOW
14	4	2	PUNCH,PUNCH	E	IN,OUT	LINK
15	4	2	SHIFT, SIDE PUNCH	S	OUT	(ALT: HAMMER)
16	5	3	KICK, PUNCH	S	IN,OUT	
17	5	3	KICK, PUNCH	S	IN,OUT	
18	5	3	KICK, PUNCH	S	IN,OUT	
19	5	3	TURN & SETUP	N	IN	
20	5	3	U-PUNCH	N	OUT	KIAI
21	0	0	YAME	N	IN,OUT	STOP

Appendix G
About The Author

I was born in 1950, and began my karate training in the summer of 1968 at Tracy's Kempo Karate in San Mateo, CA. That fall, I went to college (UCSD) and began training under Mr. Hidetaka Nishiyama (Shotokan/JKA); summer training was continued in Stanford University. Three and a half years later, I was ranked at shodan.

Upon graduation in 1972, I went to the University of Massachusetts for two years to earn my master's degree, and exchanged teaching karate for learning judo from Mr. Noriyasu Kudo, earning *sankyu* (Kodokan style) in 1973. Mr. Kudo also taught Shukokai (Tani-ha Shito-ryu) karate under the guidance of Mr. Shigeru Kimura (New Jersey). The following year was spent in Stanford University working, training karate and learning Omote-Senke Japanese tea ceremony. In 1975 I earned *nidan* from Mr. Nishiyama, and started to train with Mr. Chuck Okimura (Shotokan of Hawaii) and Mr. Isao Wada (Renshinkai). Through them I met Mr. Leroy Rodrigues (Shotokan/Shorinjiryu).

In 1976, I went to the University of Florida for the doctorate degree, taught Karate at the University Shotokan *dojo*, and trained in aikido, eventually earning *sankyu* (Yamada style) in 1980.

In January of 1981, with a newly earned Ph.D., I entered the Army (Captain, Medical Service Corps) and was stationed in San Francisco, CA. For the next four years, I trained with (and taught for) Mr. Rodrigues, earning my *sandan* and my senior instructor's certificate in the American Teacher's Association of the Martial Arts in 1984. I was then assigned to the School of Aerospace Medicine in San Antonio, and taught karate for the YWCA, as well getting introduced to kendo and kyudo.

In 1987, I left active duty to accept a faculty position as Associate Professor of Ophthalmology at the University of Kentucky. Here, after verbal promotion to *yondan* by Mr. Rodrigues, I trained in aikido for a further year (receiving *nikyu*, Saotome style in 1988) and in the Fall of 1988, started a karate P.E. class. At this time I was registered as a level C examiner by the America JKA Karate Association (Mr. Ray Dalke, Chairman). This class continues to be taught by my senior students (Pete Knox and Noel Brewer). In 1992, I was promoted to *godan* by Mr. Rodrigues; this rank was later recognized by the International Society of Okinawan/Japanese Karate-Do (ISOK) in 1994 prior to an early administrative promotion to the grade of *rokudan* in 1995 by ISOK's co-founder, Dr. Weiss, based on the *rokudan* granted by Mr. Rodrigues.

In 1997, I left the University to accept a position at Brooks Air Force Base in San Antonio, TX. Here I restricted my karate practice to training with selected senior students in an apprenticeship mode, and in 1998, was awarded the title of Renshi by ISOK, and was appointed to head the administration of ISOK a year later. I resumed training in aikido (Nishio style,) with Mr. Bill Weaver at the ShoAnJuku Dojo (Mr. Masakazu Tazaki, supervising) to further deepen my understanding of the grappling techniques hidden in the *kata* of karate-do. In addition, I started training in iaido (Soshoryu) to complement my aikido training. Further, I resumed kendo training and started training in *koryu* kenjutsu (Gomokawa Kaishin Ryu) and iaijutsu (a variant of Tamiya Ryu), both under the guidance of Mr. Tetsuzan Kuroda (Japan) to expand my knowledge of the older martial methods. Mr. Tazaki promoted me in aikido to *ikkyu* in 2000 and to *shodan* in 2001, as well as to *sankyu* in iaido. In late 2001, I moved from Texas to accept a new position at the Army Research Office in Research Triangle Park, North Carolina. Here I found a *dojo* for karate-do, and also located a kyudo *dojo* to work on the internal aspects of *budo* (currently ranked *shodan*). In 2004, I transferred the executive operating authority of ISOK to Mr. Craig Hargis, and happily reverted to teaching, giving seminars and rank examinations for ISOK when asked, while continuing to teach Shotokan karate locally, and as ancillary classes for my advanced karate students, Nishio-style aikido and Japanese sword methods (kendo kata and Soshoryu iaido). On July 19th of 2004, I received recognition from ISOK for 7th *Dan*, based on Mr. Rodrigues' recommendation, and the service title of Kyoshi.

Over the past 35+ years of training and teaching, I have been ranked in karate-do, aikido, judo, iaido and kyudo; been awarded Instructor, Senior Instructor, and Master Instructor's licenses by the American Teachers Association of the Martial Arts (ATAMA), and currently hold the grade of *nanadan* and the title of Kyoshi (ISOK). I am again teaching karate-do in a *dojo* setting as well as traveling to give private and group seminars. Finally, I maintain my aikido, kendo and iaido *kata* as well as my *koryu* sword practice and continue kyudo and cha-no-yu to maintain a balance between the active and meditative arts.

Cary, North Carolina
6 October, 2006

Also Available from Tamashii Press

"A true breakthrough in martial arts publishing!"
—Karate-do Times

For the first time in book form, HIDDEN SECRETS of karate techniques are revealed in easy-to-understand, clearly explained and illustrated sequences.

Utilizing over 330 photographs, *Bunkai*, for the first time in publishing history, allows a continuous visualization of an opponent during an enitre *kata*, without missing OR overlapping motions in the *kata* sequence. This volume covers all three *Tekki* kata: *Tekki Shodan, Tekki Nidan,* and *Tekki Sandan.*

"Carefully organized, coherent, and firmly rooted in a sense of reality. Dr. Schmeisser has done what many instructors have not yet been able to demonstrate, a cohesive and articulate interpretation of the techniques of the Tekki kata."
–Taniguchi Takao, 5th Dan, JKA Terai-machi, Ishikawa-ken, Japan

"With no wasted space on preliminaries or filler, Dr. Schmeisser dives into the subject offering unique, imaginative but nonetheless applicable interpretations of karate forms which most practitioners have heretofore justified with fanciful and non-functional explanations."
–Tony Annesi, Takeshin Sogo Budo, author of "Cracking the Kata Code"

Bunkai: Secrets of Karate Kata – The Tekki Series
By Elmar T. Schmeisser, Ph.D.

www.TamashiiPress.com

Also Available from
Tamashii Press

SHOTOKAN MASTER SEMINARS
" *Karate Training Just Like You Were There, In Person*" ™

The "Shotokan Master Seminars" series of DVDs are actual Shotokan karate seminars, conducted in various locations worldwide, and taught by some of the most highly respected and sought-after instructors. Each seminar DVD is about an hour long, and features instruction by names like:

James Yabe, Edmond Otis, Randall Hassell, and Leslie Safar

A sampling of some of our Shotokan Master Seminars titles:

- Basic Training for Youth and Adult Beginners
- Intermediate Training for 4th Kyu and Lower
- Punching Techniques: Power, Speed, & Distance
- Miscellaneous Punching Techniques
- Kata: Kanku Sho
- Awareness and Concentration
- Blocking Techniques As Attacks
- Soft Blocking

All Tamashii Press DVDs are "Region-free"

"Region-Free" DVDs are manufactured to play in DVD players and computer DVD drives worldwide. Also called "Region 0" or "Universal Format" or "Worldwide Format."

www.TamashiiPress.com

Also Available from Tamashii Press

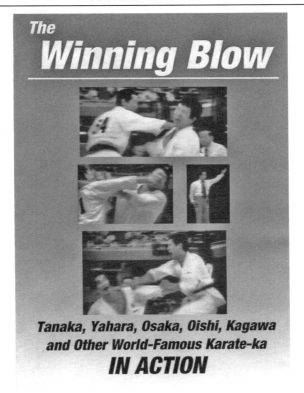

Narrated by <u>Stan Schmidt</u> of the Japan Karate Association (JKA)

See over TWO DOZEN of the world's most famous karate masters of the Japan Karate Association competing in the All-Japan Championships, training at the JKA *Honbu* (headquarters dojo) in Tokyo, and more.

This digitally restored, fast paced half-hour TV program was filmed on-location in Japan and South Africa.

www.TamashiiPress.com

Also Available from Tamashii Press

"Soul of Karate shows what the true karate spirit is about. Every instructor must see it."
--Masatoshi Nakayama, late Headmaster, Japan Karate Association

Experience the essence of traditional karate training in the rugged South African way!

Follow five karate beginners from diverse backgrounds on their challenging journey to Black Belt.

Originally shot on film, on-location in South Africa, *Soul of Karate* contains some of the most exciting karate footage ever shot! The intriguing story never lets up in this digitally restored masterpiece documentary-style movie.

www.TamashiiPress.com

*Also Available from
Tamashii Press*

"The Teacher of Teachers," Stan Schmidt, the world's highest-ranking, non-Japanese, JKA Master Instructor

provides easy-to-follow demonstrations and applications of Shotokan karate

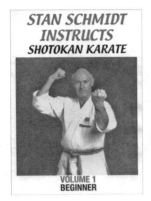
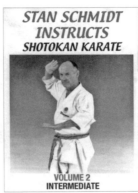
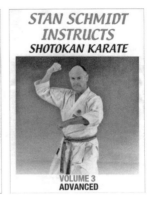

Each "Region-free" DVD contains *Kihon, Kata,* and *Kumite,* plus other level-appropriate instruction such as *makiwara,* stretching, strength and conditioning, breaking techniques, throws and holds, *gasshuku, bunkai,* and more!

Volume 1 Beginner Level
Featuring JKA World Champion Pavlo Protopappa

Volume 2 Intermediate Level
Featuring JKA World Champion Pavlo Protopappa
Special Appearance by Professional Golfer Bobby Verwey, Jr.

Volume 3 Advanced
Featuring *more than a dozen* South African National, International, and World Champions

www.TamashiiPress.com